EssaySnark's Strategies for the
2014-'15 MBA Application for
HARVARD BUSINESS SCHOOL

EssaySnark's Strategies for the 2014-'15 MBA Application for HARVARD BUSINESS SCHOOL

by EssaySnark®

Snarkolicious Press

REVISED FROM 2013 EDITION

2014 edition, version 4.1
First published May 17, 2014
Updated July 2, 2014

Snarkolicious Press
P.O. Box 50021
Palo Alto, CA 94303

www.snarkoliciouspress.com

978 1 938098 20 8

© 2011-2014 by EssaySnark®

Cover image © Eric Isselée, used under license from Fotolia.com

Look for other *SnarkStrategies Guides* (digital, paperback, and online editions) at your favorite bookseller or on the EssaySnark blahg at essaysnark.com.

Follow EssaySnark on Twitter!

"[T]he advice is fantastic. I don't know who EssaySnark is but for anyone who's looking to go to HBS, this guide is definitely a worthwhile investment!"

"MSP", HBS Class of 2013 grad, now an entrepreneur

To all the music makers,
and the dreamers of dreams.

About This *SnarkStrategies Guide*

Applying to Harvard? Awesome! So is everybody else... not to freak you out or anything.

Harvard gets well over 9,000 applications each year. Even with just one essay, with all you Brave Suppliants applying, that's still a lot for the Admissions Board to read – especially when some of you have such a way with words. More is not necessarily better with the single MBA essay at Harvard.

You need to work hard to make sure that your application doesn't suffer from some common – and avoidable – errors that can quickly move it to the "reject" pile. This *SnarkStrategies Guide* will set you up with the info you need on the most important elements of the Harvard MBA admissions process.

This *Guide* covers the 2014 application, covering the essentials that you need if you are interested in applying to this very competitive school. We have based our advice on direct observations of how Harvard responds to candidates we've worked with. We want you to use this *Guide* help you focus and hone your message, to be able to present more of what Harvard wants, while still being 100% yourself.

Please note that this *SnarkStrategies Guide* is focused on HBS's standard full-time program, not on HBS 2+2, the special program for applying to Harvard straight from college. If you're interested in 2+2, you'll still benefit from the discussion on application strategy provided here, but we're not going in-depth into tactics around when to apply and who they're looking for. As of 2014, Harvard has standardized the rounds and now any 2+2 candidate can apply during at any of the regular full-time admission deadlines.

And to set expectations right here at the front: E**ssaySnark will not tell you what to write in your Harvard essay.** Sorry. We will tell you about some avoidable errors that many people make. Plenty of Brave Suppliants will do just fine in hunkering down with these tips – plus their own first-hand research – and tackling their Harvard application. A trip to Cambridge can be incredibly useful in understanding what this school is about. If you can do so, it would be to your advantage, particularly if you can do it before you start on your application.

If you find yourself stuck on anything, we invite you to drop on over to our blahg at http://essaysnark.com or email us at gethelpnow@essaysnark.com – or even tweet us – and we'll see what we can do to help out.

Table of Contents

What Is Harvard About?

Congratulations, Brave Supplicant! By purchasing this *SnarkStrategies Guide*, you have indicated that you are taking your HBS application seriously. Cool.

Before we dive into the practical advice for all things Harvard, we have to pause and ask you: Are you ready for this?

Getting into HBS is no easy task, as we imagine you already realize. The odds are not in your favor. Why is this? Because it's an incredible place, and everybody wants to go there, so they have a lot of fine candidates to choose from. The vast majority of applicants are qualified to attend, based on the statistics of GMAT score and GPA and work experience. They have the mental horsepower and the appropriate experience to benefit from an MBA. Obviously though, the vast majority of applicants are not admitted. The ones that make it successfully through and receive an offer of admission are those who do their homework. Who know what Harvard is about, and have good reasons for wanting to go there. And, who demonstrate that they are what we call "Harvard material."

So here's EssaySnark's first question to you:

Do you know what Harvard is about?

This is an important question. And we really want to know. Take a moment and jot down your ideas on what Harvard stands for. On the things they're known for. On how they do things. What do you know about Harvard so far?

Here's even a little bit of space for you to do this. Yes, right here. Go ahead. (If you're reading this online or on your spiffy Kindle, then obviously you need to get out a pen and some paper.)

_____

_____

_____

_____

_____

_____

_____

If you felt like you couldn't come up with much, that's OK. We're going to walk you through a process to help with that. This book will teach you what to focus on. It will help you figure out where the gaps are, and investigate ways to fill them.

If the space above is blank and you could think of nothing to answer the question, then you can start by spending more time on the HBS website. Ideally you'll get the chance to go to an info session, or even better, take a trip to Cambridge and visit campus. Sit in on a class. Get to meet some students. Ask questions. Figure out what makes Harvard Harvard. What it is about Harvard Business School that makes everyone want to go there? What is exciting about the place? You need this information to do a good job on your application.

But we'll come back to that.

First:

As We Predicted: The Open-Ended Essay Is Here to Stay

For this year at least. Though we are betting that this may hang around even longer into the future.

In the 2013-2014 season, HBS introduced their single-essay application, which at the time was pretty darn radical. For a long time, Harvard has been the school leading the charge on evolving the bschool app. But this year they kept the app exactly as they did in 2013. The main reason that we believe they did this? Because there's no rules on how to approach this current question. This means that, very likely, they received some much more interesting responses. People will still try to game the system and seek to say what they think the Admissions Board wants to hear, but there's a greater chance that Harvard can get some authentic answers – and, most importantly, to see how an applicant thinks – when they have such an open-ended question.

A quick history though, because this is instructive in helping you understand where this essay question came from, and thus, how you might approach it:

For years and years, the Harvard application consisted of four essay questions. In 2012, they first shocked the system by cutting those dramatically, to just two very short essays. This apparently gave all the other schools permission to start cutting the amount of writing that they were forcing their applicants to do. The trend continued in 2013, with even more radical changes across all of the schools to their applications, set in motion by what Harvard was doing.

As you're undoubtedly aware, HBS now has just one essay. Many other schools have maintained their slimmed-down applications, though two or three questions is still the norm. No school's essays are as sparse as Harvard's – except of course for Darden, who has asked for just one main essay for many years now.

Harvard also innovated with its application through what they call the Post Interview Reflection, which was introduced in 2012. We haven't seen other schools copy that one, but there are other changes underway in terms of how interviews are conducted from school to school. The Post Interview Reflection is discussed later in this guide and it's another attempt by Harvard to get an authentic view of the applicant without all the input (or some would say, "meddling") of others – including admissions consultants.

Some takeaway messages from the Harvard approach to things:

a) The essays aren't quite as important in the application as is often assumed – the other parts of your app communicate information that's just as critical in showing who you are; and

b) Brevity is valued.

The "brevity" thing is often a sign of maturity, that you know what's important to say and how to say it, and then you know to exit. You don't outstay your welcome.

Beyond that, we'll add one more important point here at the beginning: It's important to keep in mind that *the goal with the essay (and the entire application) is to earn an invitation to interview.* You are not trying to get admitted to Harvard Business School based on the essay alone. You are trying to showcase your background and accomplishments in a way that they decide they want to meet you.

Who do they invite to interview?

Those with a track record of success.

Despite how it may appear on the surface, Harvard admissions criteria have not changed. Dee Leopold and her team are still looking for the same qualities in their candidates.

With their current slimmed-down approach with asking for just one essay, they are requesting that you focus your message to communicate who you are concisely, and precisely. Yes, it's a challenge. We're here to help you make that happen.

The Most Important Angle to Emphasize in an Application to Harvard: Leadership

Even if you've only just started your research on business schools, you probably know that leadership is a big deal at Harvard. They are focused on it pretty heavily. Their mission statement is "We educate leaders who make a difference in the world."

If you didn't already know that, then you have to dig in with those research efforts. "Harvard" and "leadership" are practically synonymous.

Leadership is the #1 most important element **of your background and profile to be highlighting for the Harvard Admissions Board.** The key criteria to determine if someone is "Harvard material" is if there's evidence that she has been a leader in a variety of contexts thus far in her life.

Or to put it another way: The HBS Admissions Board will be examining your application to look for a "habit of leadership". That's what they call it – those are their words.

OK great. So then, how do you highlight leadership? **Through IMPACT.**

In other words, how have you brought change to others?

You want everything in your application to point to this. The stories in your essay need to show that you've made a contribution in the different environments you've been in. Yes, your essay should include stories – otherwise known as examples – otherwise known as *evidence to back up your assertion that you should be admitted to Harvard Business School.*

We'll come back to that.

This "habit of leadership" also needs to ring through loud and clear in your recommendations. Whether it's at school or work, you want your application to demonstrate how you have left a place better than you found it. That you weren't satisfied with the status quo, and that you took the initiative and made the effort and instituted some changes in the wherever-you-are places that you've been.

And before we get too much further: While HBS does have a track for college kids to apply – the 2 + 2 program – they don't let those kids start the MBA until after they've had some work experience, which means the vast majority of all students roaming the halls of Harvard Business School have had a working life before ending up there. Meaning, work experience is important. Meaning, the bulk of your application materials, and probably the majority of your essay, and almost definitely your recommenders, should be pulling from your recent professional life.

Now back to the "not satisfied with the status quo" comment above: We don't mean that you should have advocated for change simply for change's sake. It's not like you sought to upend the organization or leave your fingerprints all over things just because you could. The best stories for Harvard are ones that show where you saw something that could be improved, and you did it. That's the basic model that we recommend you explore in your essay. That you had an idea for how to do things differently, and you made it happen — or maybe that others came to you to implement some important project, because they knew they could count on you to deliver. And you did.

This isn't the only way to tackle your HBS essay — we'll go through lots of different considerations for you soon – but it's not a bad place to begin your thought process, as you start doing some brainstorming around what you might want to talk about.

We'll also plant this seed for you: Dee Leopold frequently talks about how highly-qualified the majority of the applicant pool is, and that her job is about constructive a diverse class. Most people who apply meet the general requirements of the program. She is selecting a group of interesting people who will learn from each other, who will be a source of stimulation and inspiration to their peers.

If you have one goal with the essay, it's to communicate the richness of your experience in a way that shows how you will be of value to others in and outside the classroom. If you have a very unique story with unusual circumstances growing up, or you've explored far-flung territories of this planet as more than just a tourist, or you have a specifically unusual and well-developed talent that has put you in a competition position in an unusual way … these could all be worth talking about in your essay.

Oh yeah, that and the leadership thing.

What Harvard Is Looking For in Applicants

NOTE: NOBODY REALLY KNOWS WHAT HARVARD IS LOOKING FOR BUT HARVARD.

There's always all sorts of rumors and drama going through the bschool applicant community about some school or other, and Harvard is often the subject of much debate. Or lament. Or flat-out whining.

Every year, the same pattern emerges in the MBA social network gossip. Rumors go around that Harvard isn't accepting finance applicants anymore. Or because they changed their travel schedule for admissions events or interviews, that they're not going to accept candidates from [insert your country here]. Anything that Harvard does is subject to scrutiny and (mis)interpretation. There's often this lament and hand-wringing, with people complaining that well-qualified applicants have no chance at all and are categorically being shut out.

It's not true. In the years we've been doing this, we've never seen Harvard turn its back on an entire sector of their candidate pool.

Side note: How can anyone accuse Harvard of dissing Indians when in 2012 they opened a facility in Mumbai with an amphitheater-style classroom set up for the case method that looks just like the ones on the campus in Cambridge?

Please rest assured that anyone has a chance at Harvard. They don't discriminate. If you've got the chops, they want you.

Harvard is interested in a range of profiles. They seek diversity, just like every other top school. When you hear about some type of candidate getting spurned by Harvard, it's undoubtedly attributable to the sheer size of the applicant pool.

It's hard to stand out among that crowd. If you're a strong candidate who will breeze into a school like Kellogg, you simply cannot expect the same welcome in Cambridge. If you're just a *good* candidate, then it's going to be tough with HBS. You will have better luck at other schools if you're solid, and may even end up with multiple admits, but there's just no guarantees when it comes to Harvard. And, simply because a bunch of (seemingly) strong candidates of a particular type are turned away one year doesn't mean that ALL of them were. You can't go by what you read on those applicant boards. It's always a subset of candidates who are vocalizing there, and nobody has a full view of all the applicant population except for Harvard. If you have a common profile – even if yours is very strong – it's harder. The standard private equity or IB guy is going to look a lot like a gazillion other candidates on paper he'll have a tougher time standing out. But that totally does not mean that Harvard is not accepting finance guys. Or consulting chicks, or Indian dudes, or whatever category you're in that you've heard they're not accepting anymore. It just isn't true.

What is true, and what has always been true, is that it's darn tough to get into Harvard, for any type of applicant, and that fact is unlikely to change anytime soon.

But anyone telling you that Harvard isn't accepting people from finance anymore — or that they only accept kids who are 25 years old — or whatever the freak-out du jour is — they simply do not have access to the big picture. If you hear such a thing directly from Dee Leopold, then you can believe it. Otherwise? It's just rumor and hearsay and conjecture.

EssaySnark has a pretty darn good track record of success at this school. We see clients get in every year, but we don't have hugely high numbers of HBS admits to brag about — mostly because we discourage so many people from even attempting it. Harvard is for superstars. If someone approaches us who's not superstar material, no problem, we'll work with him on applications to other really good schools, like Columbia maybe, or Chicago, or Yale. Or, we work through a plan for him to *become* a superstar, and delay his app for a year. We give everyone The Talk. We show them the best way to position themselves appropriately for HBS. And, many of them do get in.

Lots of our (non-superstar) clients apply to Harvard anyway, and we do what we can to help them, too, but unfortunately, it just never works out.

For those that do get in, we are never surprised. We knew that they would. We're rarely surprised.

For those that didn't... well, we knew that, too, and we tried to tell them as much. There's a seemingly irresistible lottery mentality with Harvard though. Everyone wants to at least *try*. We get it. It's Harvard. You'll never know if you could've made it if you don't even apply. We've just never been wrong when we predicted someone wouldn't make it. We have been wrong once or twice when we thought someone had a true chance at it, but predicting a negative outcome and then someone getting in? Nope, has never happened.

Remember that this is a lot of work, and a lot of heartache, and often people turn bitter when it doesn't turn out. Just make sure you're up for the emotional rollercoaster, and recognize that it's unlikely to manifest as a win. The numbers simply aren't on your side.

If you want an opinion on how your odds might stack up, then we can do a Sanity Check for you before you submit — or, even before you start your app, you could go through the Comprehensive Profile Review, to see if your raw material might put you in the running.

We don't make Dee's decisions for her, but we're pretty confident that we can predict what she will do. We know what they're looking for at Harvard. The "habit of leadership" thing that they care about? That's pretty easy to spot. From, like, a mile away.

We're going to be talking more about this, but the primary takeaway message for you in all this is:

Snarky Strategy #1

What works at Harvard is

presenting a track record of success as a high achiever.

This has been true through the ages and it's not going to change anytime soon. There's no magic formula to this. You can show an impressive history of accomplishment while still in college, or you might be – gasp! – in your 30s already. There are no rules about age or other attributes that dictate what this looks like. And, this is going to come through in multiple places – not just your essay, but your resume, your transcripts, and your recommendations. So much so, that writing the actual essay about your accomplishments might seem almost redundant. You should have plenty of ideas for things you might cover as you go through the exercises in this guide. If you don't, well, that's could be an indication of your odds of acceptance.

One of the FAQs on the Harvard website says: "It is important for candidates to assess their own readiness when deciding to apply: there is no universal 'right' time."

What they mean is: Are you prepared to make the most of the incredible advantage that the HBS experience will afford you? Have you done something already that shows that you know how to make the most of opportunity? That you seek it out? That you're not afraid of a challenge? That you go to town and make it happen?

The other angle that they care about: Will you thrive in the case method? Are you assertive? Do you take risks?

Harvard certainly loves the *ultra-ultra* high achiever — like the Olympic athlete or founder of a thriving charity — but you don't have to be a household name (or be related to one) to get into HBS.

Also, "high achiever" is context sensitive. If you've had lots of opportunities based on privilege, birth, or lucky circumstances, then you need to show that you appreciate those opportunities and have maximized them. If you come from a less privileged background, HBS would likely also be very interested in you, based on what you've done with your circumstances. You'll need to talk about what actions you've taken and effort you've made with the chances you've had in life.

If you're in the middle — if you're a regular kid who went to a regular school and now has a regular job — you definitely have a chance too. **You just have to have *done**

something. You have to show how you're not satisfied with "regular" and you have made contributions along the way.

For example, you don't have to be the kid who spent a few years de-worming children in Africa. But, it would help if you spent a few weeks or months doing something like that — either something that was directly involved with the community, or something significant in another part of the world that was very foreign to you, that had an impact on who you are today. And you'd want to show *why* you did this. Such a story would be a way for you to illustrate something about yourself. The fact that you did a trip to work in the favelas in Brazil is less important than what motivated you to do it, and what you learned. The trip itself is just a vehicle for you to communicate what you're about to the adcom.

And please be careful with what we're saying. We're not suggesting that this type of service-based story is the most important one to use for your Harvard essay. This experience could possibly be communicated to the extent it needs to on your resume. We'll talk more later in this Guide about the best use of your limited application real estate and where you should present what to the adcom.

Also be careful about trying to "stuff" your application with such noble-sounding activities. Please do not run out tomorrow to do something that you think will impress the adcom. We knew of a BSer who quit his job and went to Nicaragua for a few months before applying to bschool – for no reason except to try and add spark to his otherwise-generic finance-guy background. There was no continuity with this to anything he'd done in the past. It didn't relate at all to his future goals. He didn't even speak the language. Needless to say, the adcom wasn't swayed. He didn't get in.

Don't be that guy. Don't look for ways to fabricate impressive-sounding stuff in your app. Work with what you've got. Show the adcom who you are – not who you think they want you to be.

Back to the high-achiever thing.

One angle to think about is *impact.* How did you leave a situation in better condition than you found it? Where did you bring in improvements that helped others?

Another potential angle is *when you took a risk.* Maybe you ditched out of a promising career in college athletics to go to work for Microsoft – or you traded your career in the pros to go into i-banking. Or your company was going bankrupt, and you decided to stay and help them turn it around, instead of jumping ship like everyone else was doing.

These examples are real students at Harvard, and some of them are former EssaySnark clients.

A quick note here to dispel a myth: You do not need to have worked at a household-name marquee-brand company in order to get into Harvard. Whether you worked at Goldman Sachs or a *barely-heard-of-'em* company is irrelevant. It just Does. Not. Matter. What does matter is what you have *done* in whatever company you've been at. What contributions you've made, what you've done to take advantage of the opportunities. How you've played the hand you've been dealt. It is irrelevant what the name of the company is.

(Side note: If it's a smaller or less-known company, be sure to include the company website URL in the Harvard application where it asks for your employment info. The Admissions Board person who will interview you will want to visit the website to learn more about it.)

So, size of company doesn't matter. Your responsibility with your Harvard application is to show the admissions committee how you've made the most of the chances you've gotten — and how you've sought out new chances when appropriate.

Why not take a moment now and write down the ways you've gone above and beyond, in whatever environment you've found yourself.

Where have you brought results to your team, your school, your company, your community?

_____

_____

_____

_____

_____

These examples might be good material to mine for the essay. Almost undoubtedly, the things you just listed out should be on your resume, if they're not already.

Speaking of which, we'll take this opportunity to issue a quick warning:

A Snarky Caveat

Your resume should be *one page only.* No matter how much fabulousness you have to report.

Yes, it's true, the online application to Harvard Business School says that you can upload a resume of one or two pages. It says that, right there on your screen. But you know what? It's not what Dee Leopold says when she's asked about it during info sessions. In the July 2014 webinar, she said, "The resume can be more than one page, but ask yourself real carefully, 'Does it need to be?'" That's a pretty broad hint.

If you're over 30, and you've accomplished a gazillion things in your career, then perhaps yes, it may be justifiable to expand your resume to a second page. Maybe. But you'd best have good reason for it, and you should also keep in mind that doing so will be emphasizing to the adcom that you are indeed older. And as we'll discuss in a moment, HBS generally prefers the younger mind that they can mold and imprint. Reinforcing your age with an endless resume may not be the best strategy. Go with a one-pager. Just do it.

Back to our discussion of the "habit of leadership" that HBS lauds....

What if you're not a high achiever?

Brave Supplicant, we implore you at this junction to be honest with yourself. About 8,500 Brave Supplicants are rejected from HBS each year. That's about 8,500 broken hearts (not to mention $200k in application fees paid out unnecessarily!). If you do not have amazing, awesome, impressive stories to present in your HBS essay... give it a think.

Sure, there's no real harm in applying (if you count "battered self esteem" and "embarrassment in front of friends and family" as "no real harm"). But it takes a big investment of time to do the essays well, and an even bigger investment of emotional energy. Take our word for it, it SUX to be rejected from any bschool.

OK, now that we've totally bummed you out... over and over again...

What do you do if you're not a high achiever? *BECOME ONE!*

Some ideas:

- Find ways to excel in your job. Be your boss's favorite person.

- Look for a problem that needs to be solved, and solve it.

- Dive in head first with your community. Roll up your sleeves and get your hands dirty.

- Take a risk.

- DO SOMETHING

And of course, it doesn't hurt if you also get an amazing score on the GMAT – though this isn't 100% mandatory to get an offer from Harvard. Plenty of kids get in with scores in the high 600s.

If now is not the right time to apply to HBS, then look for ways to build your leadership skills and create an impact in the world around you, and come up with a plan to be the type of person that Harvard would welcome with open arms *next year.*

Take a moment to take stock of your situation. Answer this one:

Why do you feel you're Harvard material? What have you done that makes you special, unique, or interesting?

_____

_____

_____

_____

Since you're hopefully starting this process early, here's another one:

What are some areas of your life where you can have more of an impact?

_____

_____

_____

_____

_____

The first list may form the basis for your entire application. The second list should spur you to action.

Just like with dating, where you keep at it until you find The One, with your MBA applications, you need to continue to work on your profile and improve yourself on an ongoing basis, from the moment you begin to think about applying, until you've got the acceptance in hand. That means, there's still opportunity for you to add to your qualifications. Use the list above to identify some tactical projects you can begin working on now, in parallel with your application. Put those in motion today.

Why is there such an emphasis on leadership at Harvard?

Harvard pumps out leaders. It's a leader-making machine. Not everyone who goes to Harvard is going to go on to rule the world, but there are some impressive HBS alumni rattling around out there.

- Michael Bloomberg, finance industry tycoon and former mayor of New York City, is a Harvard MBA.

- George W. Bush is too; so is Mitt Romney, though with his unsuccessful bid at President of the U.S., maybe he's not the best example to hold up.

- Another maybe-not-so-great one is Jamie Dimon, CEO of JPMorgan.

- But we've also got Salman Khan, founder of The Khan Academy, Michael Lynton, Chairman and CEO of Sony Pictures, Sheryl Sandberg, COO of Facebook, and Ann S. Moore, CEO of Time, Inc. – all graduates of Harvard Business School.

There are too many esteemed and notable individuals among these ranks to name them all, but hopefully you get the point. Sure, all the top bschools have lists of impressive alumni, but does any school have such an impressive list as this one? Doubtful.

The best way that the Harvard Admissions Board can predict who will come out of their program and go on to great things is to examine evidence of what you've done to date. If you have fabulous stories of go-get-'em-ness pouring out your ears already, it's much more likely that you'll be able to fulfill the potential that is expected of a Harvard MBA.

The other major reason they look for this evidence of impact is that it points to you being interesting. If you've gone out in the world and done things already, then you'll have stories to tell from it – you have experience. Even if you're younger, you have weathered some storms. This is what makes for interesting class discussions. This is what gives you the ability to make a contribution to your peers. Having something interesting to speak of based on personal experience can make you a more valued peer in the classroom and beyond. This is the key definition of "diversity" that all schools are interested in.

And a final reason that they want go-getters in the classroom: Because of the nature of the classroom itself. Harvard is not for wallflowers. It's for people who can be assertive, take a stand, form an opinion and voice it to others. That's the nature of the case method. You have to be able to argue your points in front of a room of 80 other really smart people. It is an intimidating experience. If you're a milquetoast then it's unlikely you're going to survive in that environment. HBS uses the application to screen for qualities that have proven important to success in their program.

Who is likely to be successful at Harvard? Age, GMAT, etc.

Here are just the rough generalities in terms of trends and preferences in the admissions process that we have seen to hold true at Harvard today.

1. **Age.** There is a myth that you can *only* get into Harvard if you're younger – though the definition of "younger" has been morphing at this school. Average age has fluctuated between 27 and 28 in recent years. This isn't that far off what you'll see elsewhere, except for the fact that it's the average of a much-larger class, which means that the hump of the bell curve of age at Harvard is wider – most students are closer to that general age than not. This means that most are at least a bit younger than you'll find at other schools.

HBS started a trend about seven years ago in admitting people with less work experience than other top business schools. Youngsters, even. There was a dramatic dip in students' average age (54 months of work experience average for the class of 2005, versus only 42 months in the class of 2010). For the Class of 2011, average age was about 26 (41 months of full-time work experience before entering bschool). This is quite young in comparison to many other schools.

Most recently, this trend has been reversing. Since the Class of 2012 through to 2015, the average age is 27, or about four years of post-college work experience. This compares to five years of work experience at schools like Wharton and LBS. The average age at HBS has inched up but it's unlikely to move much higher. We predict that HBS will continue to prefer applicants that have just a few years of work experience.

Harvard likes to shape young minds and imprint them with the HBS stamp. The philosophy seems to be, if you've been a superstar already in your very young life, then you can come to Harvard and shoot for the moon when you graduate.

- ***What's a "minimum" number of years of work experience?*** At least one, but probably two would be better. That's a minimum, not a maximum. This is a different metric than age because different people have different educational profiles; lots of applicants come into the MBA with a previous Master's, which means they are probably older but with less work experience.

  Harvard almost definitely will not admit you to their regular MBA program with no work experience though they could give you deferred admission (if you're still in college, apply through the 2+2 program). Having a good two years of work experience before applying to Harvard should give you more material to present in your essays as evidence of your super-star-ness. If you graduated from college in 2012, you could think about applying to Harvard this year; if you graduated in 2011, then this is most definitely your year to try. However, if you don't yet have truly impressive stories to offer about the accomplishments and contributions made on the job or in a community setting, then you'd probably be better off focusing on building up your profile and waiting a year to apply.

- **Is there a maximum?** Maybe. Harvard doesn't typically have that many students who are in their 30s. They claim to be willing to accept you even if you're in your 40s... but sorry, we just don't see it happening all that much. If you're bumping up past the 29-years-old range already, in our experience, it is tougher to get an offer at this school. It's certainly not impossible — we've seen it plenty of times — it's just not as easy. You need to show not just that you have this "habit of leadership" but you have to show even MORE of it, because you've had a longer life to accrue amazing achievements. So go ahead and apply if you're "older" — provided you're passionate enough about it — and provided you also round out your application strategy with schools that are much more interested in older candidates, such as Wharton, Columbia, Kellogg, Tuck, Haas, etc.

A note for the really young candidate:

HBS invites college students to apply through the HBS $2+2$ program.
Yale has the Silver Scholars and IESE in Spain has the Young Talent
Program, both of which also cater to current college kids. (Booth has the
Chicago Business Fellows for their part-time track which is slightly
different but still targeting the early career candidate.) HBS $2+2$ is
essentially a deferred admission: if you're accepted, you'll finish your
time at college and then go get a job for two years, maybe three, before
matriculating for a future Harvard Business School class. Stanford has the
same policy they just haven't formalized it around a specific program like
this.

A big difference between HBS $2+2$ and those two other programs is that
Harvard doesn't help you land a job; it's up to you to secure employment
following your graduation from college. And, there's a difference in
strategies for a successful $2+2$ application compared to what we're
focusing on in this Guide: For $2+2$, the adcom will want to know what
your career plans are — much more so than they typically expect or even
prefer for a regular MBA applicant. In other words, to make a go of it in
$2+2$, you'll want to explain what your goals are and why you need this
particular type of setup with guaranteed HBS in your not-too-distant
future — in order to achieve them.

It used to be that HBS only wanted candidates who wouldn't otherwise
be bschool material to apply for $2+2$. That's changed. Now it's open to
anyone and everyone — provided you're in your last year of college.

Note of course that $2+2$ is an extremely competitive track. Like,
extremely — even more so than regular HBS MBA admissions. GPAs and
test scores are incredibly high for this pool of candidates, and those who
gain an offer typically are seriously involved in their universities and in
their community, with evidence of leadership and accomplishment
abounding in their profiles. The good news about HBS $2+2$ is that you
can apply when you're still in college, and then if you don't make it in,
you can try again for the standard admissions track later, after you've
accrued some work experience. There is no stigma whatsoever with this
— you won't be blacklisted in any way if you don't make it in via $2+2$.
And, you'll know what you're up against in the HBS admissions process,
which could be an advantage for that future attempt if you decide to try
again later.

Back to the other standards that Harvard looks for.

2. **Nature of work experience.** While HBS doesn't require you to have been working for too many years before applying, and there isn't any one industry that's better than another, **the nature or quality of the work and the contributions made there need to be significant.**

   As we've been saying, the adcom wants to see evidence of achievement and impact in order to admit you. That impact can come in any context – they most definitely are open to nontraditional work experience, including the Peace Corps, nonprofit work, and the military. They'd likely love to see an application from, say, an elementary school teacher, or a pharmacist, or a firefighter. Someone not from the traditional ranks of business. Anyone with that type of unusual profile will get extra attention.

   Note though that they can only admit so many people in each category, and they're getting a massive influx of applications from you military guys. If you're a military chick applying to bschool, you'll be at a great advantage, as there are so few of you. The military dudes are becoming ever more common though. It used to be fairly "easy" – if there is such a thing as "easy" with a HBS application – for a military candidate to get in, but this has changed due to the sheer volume of candidates in this category. If you're military, or any oversubscribed pool of candidate, you should try to apply in Round 1 to help your chances.

   EssaySnark has a bunch of special support services for military candidates – please go to http://essaysnark.com/military-mba/ to learn more.

   Also as we mentioned earlier, lots and lots of your stereotypical bschool candidates are admitted to Harvard each year. By "stereotypical" we mean simply that they're coming from private equity or Wall Street or big-name consulting firm. By "stereotypical" we DON'T mean that they're average or plain vanilla. The point is, if you're coming from a more traditional industry, you absolutely can have a chance at Harvard if you have enough stories of … wait for it... *leadership and impact.* So again, go for Round 1, and be sure you trot out the interesting stuff in those essays.

3. **GMAT.** HBS doesn't care if you have a GRE score instead of a GMAT score, but if you haven't tested yet, you should just suck it up and do the GMAT. Most people feel that the GMAT is a harder test – which is exactly the reason why you should do it. This is Harvard we're talking about, remember? Go for the big challenges. It'll help you in demonstrating your qualities.

If you already have a decent GRE score and it'll be valid at the time you'll be applying, you should feel confident in submitting that. We don't get many clients with GREs though, so we'll discuss test score qualifications based on the GMAT, simply because we know a lot more about it. Most bschools don't publish GRE averages since they don't have enough data on them (which again should tell you that you should do the GMAT instead). One exception is HBS 2+2 where you can see averages for successful applicants for both the GMAT and the GRE test, in case you're in that applicant pool. If you'll be applying with a GRE, regardless of what candidate pool, then you should look for the 2+2 class profile and compare your test score with the averages reported for those successful applications.

Let's talk about Harvard and GMAT scores.

The median GMAT for HBS students is a stratospheric 730. Freak you out yet? Don't worry, HBS is actually more accommodating on the GMAT front than you might expect. Because of its large class size – 940 students these days – wow! – Harvard can absorb students with a range of scores — particularly those coming from the nontraditional areas mentioned above like military or Peace Corps etc. However, a higher GMAT score is most definitely going to help you in a Harvard application. This is particularly true for younger candidates; you need to prove that you're a go-getter and one way you can do that is through a strong GMAT.

Here's a set of sobering statistics:

- 50% of the HBS Class of 2009 scored between 700 and 740 on the GMAT

- 50% of the Class of 2010 scored between 700 and 750; and

- 50% of the Class of 2012 scored between 710 and 750.

(They've unfortunately stopped releasing the 50%-range in recent years.)

Sure, that means that in the 2009 admissions season, about 450 students either scored between 760-790, or between 510-710. That year they admitted one person with a really really really low GMAT — previous years, the bottom score has rarely dipped below 570. But with an average GMAT of 724 that year, then most definitely there were not that many students — maybe not more than the one — in the lower realms.

The trend is for higher scores – but the truth is that *Harvard looks at the underlying components more than totals.* This should hopefully help you see the importance of the GMAT at HBS. The common wisdom applies: A higher score won't guarantee you'll get in, but a lower score could keep you out – and it's not just about getting a 700+. You need to demonstrate proficiency on all dimensions.

4. **GPA.** Harvard is a little less hung up on GPA for older applicants (in the 28- to 29-year-old range) but grades definitely do matter, for the same reason as everything else we've been saying.

   If you're younger – like, still in school, or just graduated – then academics are expected to be one key area where you've been an outperformer. It's sort of hard to justify accepting someone to this type of high-end graduate program if they just finished out their undergraduate career with lackluster performance; poor grades in college basically indicates you don't care about school much, so why would you care about it at Harvard? You'll have a tough time getting in if you're young with a low GPA. If you're older it may be less of an issue, though it's never a non-issue. If your GPA is really low, that can definitely keep you out of Harvard (other schools, too).

   The average GPA has recently been a very high 3.67. Harvard is an academically rigorous place, and they need to know you can cut it in the classroom. A good GPA also shows that you value education, which basically says that you'd appreciate the opportunity to go to Harvard.

   Yes, a high GMAT can help out if your GPA is on the low side – a little. It can't compensate if your academics were really poor but it can give your chances a boost if they're borderline.

   No matter what, you're going to have a tough time if your GPA is below 3.0. And it's highly unlikely you'll make it through the screening process if both your GPA and your GMAT are below average (unless you're a U.S. minority; many schools make exceptions to their standard requirements in certain cases, in an effort to offer more opportunities to underrepresented populations).

   We cover ideas for how to counter a low GPA or GMAT score on our blahg at http://essaysnark.com. The one addition we'll offer specific to HBS is a change made to the 2014 app, where they have a section asking for non-degree coursework. They'll let you list out any unaccredited programs such as MOOCs (Coursera, Udacity, etc.). Other schools may not give much weight to these but HBS is putting a push behind its own online initiative and so is more receptive to this format as proof of interest and abilities.

   Also: Do not try to convert your academics to the U.S. 4.0 scale if that's not how your school has recorded it. Just leave the GPA field blank. The adcom is very familiar with grading systems and scales from schools all around the world. They'll be able to deal with it.

5. **English proficiency.** The TOEFL is required if you did not do your undergrad in an English-speaking university, and it's recommended even for some candidates who may not need to submit the TOEFL for other bschool apps. Be sure to study each school's requirements carefully. (Fun fact: Dee Leopold is the first one to read incoming emails sent to the general inquiry Harvard system. She reports that "Do I have to take the TOEFL?" is the #1 question they receive, followed by "Do I have to take the GMAT?" The answers to both these questions are easily found on the Application Requirements page of the HBS website.)

    Silly thing to say but: If your profile dictates that you need to take it, then you need to do well on the TOEFL. Harvard clearly discourages anyone who doesn't perform well on the TOEFL or other language test from even applying – it's one of the only areas in which they offer this type of discouragement, so you can assume they're serious about not budging on an admission decision for someone who doesn't have their language chops in line. (And if you didn't understand that sentence... maybe you need more practice with idioms and the oddities of English.)

6. **International Experience.** While this isn't a mandatory component of an application, in recent admissions seasons, we saw that those with a significant international profile and even ex-pat work experience were exceptionally appreciated by the Harvard adcom. This fits in with Dean Nohria's emphasis on global business and his commitment to strengthening the school's reach beyond the U.S.

    One stereotype of an applicant profile is someone who grew up in an Asian country, came to America for grad school, and has been working here a few years. While this certainly does fit the definition of "international experience", it's so commonplace that it's almost a cliché. If you're Indian or Chinese or Korean, and you've worked in the U.S. or Canada *as well as* somewhere in Europe, or perhaps in South America, or somewhere else more unusual (Middle East?), then you'd have a big leg up on the other Asians who are also applying.

    Any significant international work experience should be considered as a potential essay topic for Harvard. What we mean by that is, if you've spent time as an ex-pat, or even just on an extended business trip, look to that time and those circumstances and that project to see if you have any good examples of achievement to pull from. See if you have a story to tell that uses the backdrop of your time in-country to highlight those experiences.

    The standard undergraduate study-abroad experience that many American college students undertake is not what we're talking about here. Much better would be to focus on time you've spent living and working in some other country in recent years, and what you did there, and even how it affected you. Or, if your career goals involve some type of international business or endeavor overseas (such as the IMF or

World Bank etc.), then this can also help you satisfy this interest of the HBS adcom (as long as it's genuine and authentic! do not make stuff up just because you think it's what they want to hear).

These are broad-strokes guidelines, not set-in-stone rules for what Harvard wants and how they'll react to a given profile. You'll want to study the requirements listed out on the HBS website and make sure you are meeting them, both the letter and the spirit of what Harvard is looking for.

Common Myths About HBS Admissions

Here are some untruths that are often bandied about as "facts" on what Harvard is (or isn't) looking for in their candidates' profiles.

To reiterate: These statements are NOT TRUE.

1. **Only the Rich and Famous get in.**

   HBS is still an old boys' club to some degree; there was a set or articles that came out in the *New York Times* in September 2013 that underscores this fact. Yet many students refuted the claims made by the reporter. You can see those articles and EssaySnark's reaction to them on our Harvard page on the site (under the Essay Questions menu). Regardless of who you believe, we have firsthand experience that proves that connections can matter. Who you know can give you an edge in getting in. But it's most certainly not exclusively that. You definitely do not need to have a rich uncle or a politician father to get an offer at Harvard. And, name-dropping can sometimes *hurt*. Sure, if you happen to have a good relationship with a well-connected alumnus at the school, it can be very strategic to work that into your application. But getting a letter of recommendation, for example, from a famous person who doesn't actually know you is just sort of dumb. They won't be able to say anything useful about who you are and what your strengths are. This will not help you. Use any relationships that you have in terms of connections to the school, but don't manufacture or invent them if they're not there. And if your dad's college roommate's sister's brother-in-law takes his dog to the same vet that Mitt Romney took his dog after strapping him to the roof of the car for the family vacation – if you're not following U.S. politics then sorry you won't know what we're talking about here.... anyway if you are 16 times removed from some famous person, don't bother trying to work that tenuous connection get them to write a letter for you. It'll do nothing for your chances at Harvard.

2. **You have to have gone to a fancy college to get in.**

   Despite the common belief to the contrary, you need not have gone to an Ivy League school to get into Harvard. They want to see how you made the most of your college experience and leveraged it for success — whether it was at a small liberal arts college, a regular state school, or a three-year degree in India. Want proof? Check out the list of schools that recent students have come from:

   http://www.hbs.edu/mba/admissions/admission-requirements/Pages/undergraduate-institutions.aspx

   If your school is on the list, you're in good shape, and even if it's not, it's not necessarily a problem. Remember, they like diversity, and undergrad institution is one angle that shows you're from a different background than other students.

Of course, if you went to a high-end college, then that can hint at a history of working hard, even way back from high school. You could not have made it into a very selective undergrad unless you worked your bootie off as a kid. So it can count. It's just not a binary decision on the Admissions Board's part.

3. **You can get into Harvard with a really low GMAT.**

Unfortunately, another myth surrounds how likely it is to get into HBS with a low GMAT score. On many bschool discussion boards, people seem to latch onto the rumors and stories about some person they heard of who got in with a 520 GMAT. These cases are very, very rare. Like, there's ONE person each year who pulls this off. (That's 1 out of about 9,500 applications. Or 0.01% of applicants. Just as a reminder.)

The fact of the matter is, if your GMAT is below, say, 660, it is **highly unlikely** that you will get an offer from Harvard. The exceptions are if you're from an underrepresented group like African-American or Hispanic (or *really* underrepresented like American Indian or Eskimo), in which case many schools will be actively courting you, provided your work history and career goals are in decent shape. As already discussed, the average GMAT at HBS is incredibly high, and they do not make many allowances for candidates with subpar scores except in very rare cases.

We've already explained that Harvard looks for achievement, and one easy category for them to see evidence of that is in the GMAT score. Having a low score undermines your argument that you're an overachiever.

4. **You can easily get in with a high GMAT.**

You may be surprised to learn that many of the best bschools REJECT a huge number of the highest-scoring candidates. This is true at Harvard as well. Every year, when EssaySnark reviews the profiles of Brave Supplicants who do not get in, very frequently we find that it's the top-scoring applicants who are left without an offer. Why? We have many theories, the strongest is simply that these 760+ GMAT holders suffer from hubris and arrogance. They are often highly accomplished, frequently coming from the best name firms on Wall Street or in consulting, and they just come across as, well, jerks in their essays. We do our very best to help them not sound like jerks in their essays, but there's only so much we can do – and sometimes, if they really are a jerk, then we let them go ahead and be themselves.

**5.	You can get in during Round 3.**

We're already going on and on about how hard it is to get into Harvard. Do you really think that it's going to be any easier during Round 3? The Harvard Admissions Board even recommends that most people don't apply then! (They've said it in their webinars, including one that as of this writing – May 2014 – is available as a video on their website.) Unfortunately though, they're not consistent with this message. We ranted about this on the EssaySnark blahg in March 2014: http://essaysnark.com/2014/03/everybody-likes-choices/ Bottom line: We *really* don't think you should try in Round 3. Sit back, relax, and put your sights on Round 1 in the coming season. Your chances will be infinitely better.

6.	**If you're Indian, it's really hard to get into Harvard.**

This is also not quite true – except that it's hard for everyone. A fairer characterization might be that if you're *an engineer who happens to be Indian* it's tough to get in, only because there's so gosh darned many of you trying. HBS doesn't care so much what your ethnicity is, they care what your personal and professional profile looks like. They actually admit a lot of engineers though, so that fact alone is not a problem.

The problem is that the Indian IT candidate (or other type of engineer-by-training) is unfortunately a dime a dozen in terms of bschool apps, and on paper, many of you guys look the same. There's no problem with you coming in as an Indian; what you need to do is show how you're differentiated – which is exactly the same thing that everyone else needs to show. The key question you need to address in your app is, how will you bring a different perspective to the Harvard classroom and community? HBS is pretty friendly to engineers, so believe it or not, you have a leg up – they recognize that an engineering mindset means you'll be good at the math stuff that they teach. If you're an engineer with a lower quant GMAT score, by the way, then that's not going to be so appealing to them. No matter what, just like with everyone, you need to present stories of achievement and impact in order to show why they should accept you over all those others.

What's our point? We want you to recognize that Harvard looks for the same type of applicant that many other good bschools look for — except that with Harvard, they're sorting through double (or triple) the number of applications looking for those attributes. The signal-to-noise ratio is low. And they have high standards. You need to work hard to stand out at Harvard.

What does "stand out" look like?

Well, circling back to our invitation at the beginning of this guide for you to define what leadership means, why not re-examine the qualities that you came up with there, in light of this post from the Harvard student newspaper:

http://www.harbus.org/2013/samba-awards-november-2013/

The key quote? "Where others might say 'I feel like I should do something,' Elsa decides, takes action, and leads." You just *know* that her application was chock-full of evidence that that's how she lived her life.

Do you have any examples like that? You'll want to use them in your Harvard application.

What Not to Do

Let's start talking in specifics. Here's a short list of things to avoid in your Harvard pitch. When writing your essay:

- **Do not speak in generalities.** Don't talk about how you finished a project and impressed your client, and thus got a promotion. Instead, tell the adcom reader what you *did*. It's very, very important to be specific in describing how you brought change to the organization or what you literally did to get something done. The reader needs to see evidence of your skills and abilities through the stories you choose, and through how you tell them. This is true for all schools, but perhaps even more so for Harvard. You should also coach your recommenders to do this.

- **Do not fawn.** What we mean by this is, you should not make it sound like you think HBS is God. You should not write gooey sticky prose that talks about how great the school is or how much you have wanted to go there since you were ten.

  Similarly, you should not be boastful about your own self. HBS gets plenty of applications from arrogant full-of-themselves snobs, and it's a real turn-off to have to wade through any of that in an essay.

  Everyone wants to go to Harvard; you don't have to say that it's been your lifelong dream. It's more important to demonstrate why they should accept you. A dream to go to Harvard is meaningless in the context of the competitive admissions process. Again, use specifics when you write, just like we said in the previous bullet about how best to present your experiences. *Specifics, people.* Specifics.

- **Do not abbreviate.** Here we mean a few things. The first one is perhaps just EssaySnark's preference and not a rule, but we think applicants should not say "HBS" in their essays. It's too familiar. Use the full school name wherever possible (we think you should do this in all your essays, to any school) – or at a minimum, say "Harvard."

  More importantly, avoid all acronyms. Those are almost always jargon and they make it harder for a reader to go through your essay. The only ones you can safely use would be standard terms like CEO or ROI. You also need to rework your resume to replace NPV and IRR and EM with plain English terms, and please don't let any of those abbreviations sneak into your essay.

- **Do not be sloppy.** If you don't proofread your HBS essay with exceptional care, you may set yourself up for failure. Even one single typo can be the kiss of death. No, if you're a superstar candidate that they really want, they will not reject you because of a typo. (Probably.) But there will be plenty of other superstars whose essays are perfect. Take your time with the Harvard application. Make it shine.

Other Harvard application don't-do advice:

- **Do not switch to the GRE as a "trick" if your GMAT is low.** If you've tested the GMAT and are worried your score isn't high enough, do not try to use the GRE instead. While HBS and many other schools will accept a GRE score, it's got a reputation as being easier than the GMAT. The GMAT is one doozie of a test. HBS says they're agnostic and neutral and you can submit either test, but don't be fooled into thinking you can game the system by going with the GRE because you did lousy on the GMAT. Remember that when converted, a high GRE score often looks like a less-impressive GMAT equivalent. If you're having trouble, sorry but you're just going to have to keep studying. Retake the GMAT and do better.

  The one exception here might be if you're a 2+2 applicant, in which case the GRE could work fine for you. We mentioned another exception on our blahg; see http://essaysnark.com/2011/06/the-one-case-ok-maybe-two-when-the-gre-makes-sense/ . Generally, the GMAT is the way to go if you've got bschool in your future.

- **Do not write an optional essay.** You can't write one, actually. HBS doesn't allow it. You need to plan to cover all the elements of your profile — including any missteps or glitches in your academics, a gap in employment, and anything else — in the standard application assets. As an example, sometimes there's a way to explain on your resume how you spent your time in the five months when you were backpacking through Europe after college, before you started your first job. There's also lots of fields on the application itself, and sometimes you can fit the necessary information into one of them in a logical way, to explain an oddity in your background that needs explaining. There's also one spot on the application to offer "additional information" but it's a pretty small field (in recent years they've allowed only 500 characters — that's *characters*). In the July 2014 webinar, Dee Leopold was pretty clear that this is not another essay. It's meant to explain anything in your history that might need explaining, that isn't obvious on its surface.

  If you've written an optional essay for another school and are trying to figure out where to fit that information into your HBS application, you'll either need to get creative and see if the topic you covered can be appropriately positioned in the HBS essay – though we are not keen on that as a strategy. Or, you'll need to be very brief in that Additional Information application field.

- **Do not worry about applying early.** While it's always wise to get your application in before the day of the deadline, to avoid the traffic jam on the school's servers and any technical glitches, and corresponding major stresses, that may arise, there is no benefit to submitting a Harvard application early. Some schools encourage you to submit early. Harvard doesn't care. You get no special brownie points for submitting a month early versus on the last day. They're even pretty flexible about situations where a recommender submits the recommendation a day or so late.

That being said, you do not want to procrastinate with your Harvard app, since crafting this essay will take many rounds of revision – probably more than any other schools' essays will need. You need to give yourself time for that in-depth process. Plan on spending at least a month doing rewrites, and then get the application completed by September 1st or so – you are applying in Round 1 aren't you? Oh, right. If you came to this game a little late, just get your Round 2 app in before the holidays in December so you don't have to worry about it when you're drinking your yuletide cheer. The advantage is not that your app will be evaluated early, or that you'll be in a better position with admissions because you have your app done sooner. The advantage is to you in minimizing stress. Because there will be stress. Count on it.

Let's go back to that rewriting thing.

We sorta implied this just now but may as well state it upfront: Even though there's only one essay, and you can write about anything you want, and make it as long as you want, this does not mean that your HBS application will be the easiest one to knock out.

In fact, it may well become the hardest, due to exactly those factors.

You'll need to do a significant amount of brainstorming, and reflection, and hammering out and reworking your message, in order to develop a robust, comprehensive, yet concise application theme that can carry you into Harvard. Once you do that, then you will likely be in very good shape to apply to other schools, just based on the amount of work you'll need to do in order to come up with a compelling pitch for the HBS Admissions Board.

Some Macro Strategies

That leads us into a discussion of timing and planning. Let's start with this:

Snarky Strategy #2

Since you're applying to multiple schools —
because you're smart, and you know that you
cannot count on an offer from HBS — you
may want to write the essays for at least one
other school first.

Before we get too far on that idea, we need to also caution you:

A Snarky Caveat

YOU CANNOT USE THE ESSAYS YOU WRITE FOR OTHER SCHOOLS FOR HARVARD.

Apologies for the all-caps screaming but we need to make this point crystal clear.

Don't reuse other essays for HBS. No recycling. Lots of people will do this. Lots of people will be making a big mistake when they do.

All the schools are aware of what their peer programs are asking in the essay questions. Harvard knows full well what Stanford and Wharton and MIT and Kellogg are asking. If they get even a whiff of an idea that you have re-used an essay written for one of those schools' questions for your single HBS essay, well.... that's not gonna go over too good.

However, in many cases, the hard work you put into writing your essays for those other schools will:

a) Teach you something important, namely: how to write an essay

b) Help you uncover the pieces and parts of your profile that are the most important to present

The best example? Yale's 2014 essay question, that asks you to talk about how you have "positively influenced an organization."

Hmmm, where have we heard that before?

Oh yeah. We told you that that's what you should be focusing on for Harvard. So clearly you've got some synergistic opportunity right there. But it doesn't mean you get to do a save-as on your SOM essay and slap it up onto the HBS server.

While you may be tempted to do your Harvard essay first, since it's the first deadline, we are going to suggest that maybe you hold off. You may find that it's easier to do things in reverse.

Why? Three main reasons:

1. We already said that Harvard gives you no brownie points for submitting early. So in the interest of managing the overall project of applying to multiple schools, it may make sense to prioritize other schools first.

    Remember, if you're also applying to Columbia in the Early Decision or J-Term cycles, then you should most definitely do that application first (but you already knew that, since you've devoured the *SnarkStrategies Guide for Columbia*, right?).

    Of course, if you're applying to Columbia during the ED round, then you really should not be applying to Harvard during their Round 1, because a Columbia ED app is an advance commitment to go to Columbia if they accept you... and we'd hate to see someone in the situation of having been accepted to Columbia right when HBS has issued an interview invite. That would mean the person would need to pull the plug on their promising Harvard application in order to make good on their commitment to Columbia. To reneg on Columbia in that situation is way sucky and we think you are a big-time jerk-o if you would do that. So probably you won't be applying to Columbia ED if you're reading this *Guide*, right? Right.

    [Off soap box]

2. The other reason to do other schools' essays first? Learning how to write an essays *on other schools' questions* will likely result in you having a much stronger HBS essay when you turn your attention there. Writing bschool essays is not an easy task. Most people aren't good at it until they've been wrestling with it awhile. Believe us, we know, we have seen people struggle with this stuff for years. You will benefit in a bunch of ways by cutting your essay-writing teeth on another schools' drafts to begin with. Similarly, you will want to interview with other schools before going for the all-important HBS interview, so lining up a Tuck or a Duke or a Kellogg interview early in the season is exceptionally wise.

3. There's a third reason for wading through a different school's essays before doing Harvard's: Having a strong understanding of what your career goals are, through

hammering out a career goals essay like Columbia or Tuck asks, will actually help you with Harvard – *yes, even though Harvard doesn't have a career goals essay.*

The reason? Because it will inform all the decisions you make on what to write about for the main HBS essay. If you know your career goals, then you should have clearer insights and sharper understandings about what type of experiences to choose and stories to tell to Harvard; you will pick examples that resonate with and better reinforce your messaging around the whole pitch, including the goals which are just briefly described.

(You hopefully are already aware that Harvard does ask about goals. It's in the online application. Oh? You did not know this? Hm. Well maybe you should sign onto their application and check things out.)

We're getting ahead of ourselves on these essay strategies, but this is important stuff and we want you to think about the big picture of your overall approach in the best way possible.

Planning for recommendations

Since we're talking about which order you should do which thing, here's another important idea to consider:

Snarky Strategy #3

Don't hit up your recommenders until after you have written essays for at least one school.

Just get one set of essays done. They don't have to be Harvard's. Then set your recommenders loose on their task.

Why not get your recommenders on board first, before you tackle the HBS essay? After all, that part is easy, right? You're basically outsourcing it. You could go talk to your recommenders and get them started, and feel all smug and self-satisfied, like you're making great progress on your application. But every element of your HBS app is an opportunity for you to be *strategic*, and one strategy that many people miss out on is leveraging the recommendations in conjunction with the rest of their application.

This is even more important in this Brave New World of a single essay, with no precise question to answer.

You need all components of your application to work together. You need your recommenders to be covering specific topics on your behalf – you aren't going to dictate what they say, but recommenders often appreciate it when the applicant suggests some things to write about. Your recommenders can add value in a very targeted way if you approach them correctly. And usually, that means approaching them *after* you know what your application theme is. Which, usually, you cannot have established fully until after you've developed out the essay to at least draft 2.

This especially important when your one Harvard essay is completely freeform. You need to devise *an application strategy* to convey all aspects of your fabulous self to the adcom. The recommendations have always been important – people often do not realize how important they are. The adcom says as much in the essay prompt – they mention that you're already communicating who you are to them through the recommendations and resume and all. You must leverage the opportunity that your recommenders have in presenting the adcom with more, and more detailed, information and insights about who you are as a candidate. But you can effectively do that only if you already know what you're going to say about yourself through your own writing in that essay.

What EssaySnark suggests is, **get through at least the first couple drafts of your essay for your first school before talking to your boss about writing any recommendations.** *Then you'll know where the holes are in your profile, and you can suggest ideas for what your boss can talk about that can fill those holes.* At least, they can do that in the first recommender's question. They can't do that in the second one, since that's a very specific query that they'll need to address head-on (it asks for them to describe a time when they gave you constructive feedback).

Remember, just as they indicate in the essay prompt, the Harvard adcom is going to look at your application as a whole. All the pieces must work together. And, you can be strategic about how the different elements work *off of* each other.

As you're developing your material, you will have to make choices between which topics to cover in your essay. Maybe you're choosing between a story about project you did at work last year, or this other one about this volunteer thing you led. If you're designing your essay BEFORE your recommenders have written their letters about you, you have a lot more room for optimizing the equation.

You could, for example, decide to use the volunteer thing in your essay, and ask your boss to talk about the project from work. That way, the adcom gets both sides of you presented.

IMPORTANT: This example allocation of material – work vs. volunteer story – may or may not be the right way to go FOR YOU. The HBS adcom actually wants to see mostly work-related stories – so please do not interpret this little example as *advice* that you should always choose a volunteer story for your essay. That is not at all what we're saying here.

Back to your recommender strategy:

If you've already had the "what should I write about" discussion with your boss, then it may be tough to go back and ask her to redirect her efforts.

However, this is a pretty crucial tactic for you to take advantage of. It can help the school see more aspects of who you are, and it can give you a little more control over how you're presenting. Note, too, that such "what should I write about" conversations with your recommenders are perfectly fine, as long as you don't actually write the recommendations yourself!! We don't need to tell you that that is unethical. It's often fairly easy for an astute adcom member to detect a candidate-written rec, believe it or not. And yes, that alone is grounds for rejection. Don't do it, it won't pay off.

So: Write your HBS essay first – or even better, get through the full set for one of your other schools' essays. Then go talk to your recommenders about what they might be able to say about you.

Like most schools, HBS requires two recommendations (up through 2012, they asked for three). You should have at least one, and preferably both, of those recommenders come from a direct supervisor in a professional setting. There's lots of variability in terms of who to ask and how to strategize, but the bottom line is that they both need to be speaking to your "habit of leadership" in different contexts and through different opportunities. If you want more guidance on strategies for who to choose, check out the EssaySnark App Accelerator on Letters of Recommendation, available on our website.

OK. We know what you're thinking. "EssaySnark, when are we going to get to that essay?"

Soon, Brave Supplicant. Let's cover something else important first.

Harvard and Career Goals

As we already stated, your track record as a LEADER is critical for how you present to HBS. And if you've read through the *SnarkStrategies Guide* on Columbia, you may be wondering about the difference in emphasis. In a Columbia application – as in a Wharton application, and many other schools – the CAREER GOALS are the most important angle.

Not so at Harvard.

The career goals do matter at Harvard – but as Dee Leopold has been saying repeatedly lately, they don't want to see "a laminated life plan." That is a turn-off to them, mostly because they feel that bschool is going to be so transformational that you probably don't have a clue what you actually will want to do as you move through the process.

But at least directionally, you need to be able to describe your future plans for the adcom. You need to have a reason for being interested in business school. The answer to that question goes in a tiny little field in the online application, and it may come up in the interview. Your goals can be discussed in the essay, if you choose. But they shouldn't be the main focus.

Harvard isn't obsessed about career goals. Certainly nothing like the way those other schools are.

Part of this is simply a dose of reality: HBS know that very few people will do what they state they're going to do on their bschool essays.

As well, it's due to the premium that this school places on the HBS experience. They know that it is completely transformative. They know that you will come out of their program a very different person. Remember, they call it a "transformative education." So while it may be fair game for you to talk in the essay about where your interests lie and why you feel a Harvard MBA would help you get to the next level (or two) in your life, they are not that hung up on getting a complete dissection of your career goals as the mainstay of your application.

If you're applying to a school like Columbia or Berkeley that is laser focused on the career goals, *it would still make sense to develop your answer to that question for that application first, before trying to come up with a Harvard essay strategy.* The effort that you'll have to exert in defining your career goals specifically for the Wharton or Kellogg questions will take you far in positioning yourself for Harvard,

So to reiterate: Despite the seeming de-emphasis on career goals at HBS, they are still important. An MBA is still a professional degree, and you need to know at least directionally why you want one, in the context of what you want to do with your life. Even more important is to understand why you want one from *Harvard*.

And don't forget: If you're going for the $2+2$ application, as we said earlier, it will be more important for you to be specific on the future and why you need this special $2+2$ format and program to get where you want to go.

And oh yeah: Many times, career goals do come up as a line of questioning in the interview. They're not irrelevant.

Harvard and the wanna-be entrepreneur

We can't talk about Harvard and career goals without talking about Harvard and entrepreneurship. Obviously this is a big push at this school now, as it is at all the top MBA programs. Entrepreneurship is sweeping the nation! It seems that everyone and his brother wants to start a company. The number of applicants who say they're interested in entrepreneurship has exploded just in the past two years.

If you want to go to Harvard for entrepreneurship, great – but please, be very careful about how you talk about that in your essay.

If you have any kind of entrepreneurial experience already, then you're going to want to leverage that through your application assets, most likely on both the resume and in the essay as well.

If you don't... well, it's going to be tough for the adcom – any adcom – to see how you're qualified as an entrepreneur. It's not impossible to get admitted to a top MBA program with a set of entrepreneurial goals if you've never done any type of startup yourself, but it's definitely not the easiest way to go. If you have hopes and dreams of launching your own business at some point in the future but it's not in the near-term game plan, then perhaps just leave it out of the essay entirely? If it's something you plan to do straightaway after bschool, then we'd recommend integrating that plan into the essay itself. Convince the adcom of what you want to do, by providing evidence of what you've done in the past that's relevant, to show that you're ready to make it happen for yourself.

Entrepreneurial goals are tricky. Lots and lots of people are applying to bschool with goals like that these days. The schools are embracing on a massive scale, in terms of programs and resources and support for their students who want to be entrepreneurs. But it doesn't mean that it will be any easier to get *in*to bschool with such goals. If that's your plan, we strongly recommend getting it vetted before going too far with it.

Now we're ready. Let's talk about that Harvard essay.

The Harvard MBA Application Essay

We mentioned earlier that Harvard has never changed what they're looking for in applicants. They've simply changed how they're looking, through changes to the application over the years.

In other words, with this single-essay application, they're letting you take control of your destiny. Instead of have you work like a robot to sweat through predefined essay prompts, they're turning the reins over. You're in control.

This helps you present a more authentic self to them, since there's no one "right answer". The essay question is completely open-ended. How could there be just one way to handle it? This allows them a chance to see how you think. It's a strategic exercise on your part.

It also helps them by minimizing (hopefully!) the amount of stale, cookie-cutter responses. There's lots of books and websites out there that tout "Winning essays from Harvard!" The adcoms must detest those. Dee Leopold has even commented disparagingly about them in the past. A key reason why we don't publish successful essays on our site is because we realize that the temptation would be too great. People would crib from them – as they undoubtedly crib from those books with "winning essays!" that litter the Internet.

How, then, are we going to steer you in the right direction? If we're not going to give you samples of what to write, then what's the point of us publishing a Harvard essay guide?

Very simple. We're going to help you understand what HBS is looking for – just as we've been doing, with all the talk about leadership and achievement. And we're going to walk you through some of the questions that Harvard has asked in past years.

Those will serve you well, in understanding what Harvard is looking for.

We're not suggesting that you should answer this year's essay question exactly as if it were one from a past year. What we're doing is letting you see what Harvard has asked before, so you get a sense of what matters to them.

We're also going to share with you how Harvard's professors evaluate their students in the classroom – because that will give you insight into what they expect to see in their applicants.

First though, let's look at what they literally asked people to present in essays of years gone by.

Past Harvard essay questions

2012 Admissions Season

Two questions:

1. Tell us about something you did well. (400 words)
2. Tell us about something you wished you'd done better. (400 words)

2011 Admissions Season

Four questions:

1. Tell us about three of your accomplishments. (400 words)
2. Tell us three setbacks you have faced. (400 words)
3. Why do you want an MBA? (400 words)
4. Answer a question you wish we'd asked. (400 words)

2010 Admissions Season

Four questions:

1. What are your three most substantial accomplishments and why do you view them as such? (600 words)
2. What have you learned from a mistake? (400 words)
3. Please respond to two of the following (400 words each):
   - What would you like the MBA Admissions Board to know about your undergraduate academic experience?
   - What is your career vision and why is this choice meaningful to you?
   - Tell us about a time in your professional experience when you were frustrated or disappointed.
   - When you join the HBS Class of 2013, how will you introduce yourself to your new classmates?

2009 Admissions Season

Four questions:

1. What are your three most substantial accomplishments and why do you view them as such? (600 words)
2. What would you like us to know about your undergraduate academic experience? (400 words)
3. What have you learned from a mistake? (400 words)
4. Please also respond to one of the following (400 words each):
   - Discuss how you have engaged with a community or organization.
   - What area of the world are you most curious about and why?
   - What is your career vision and why is this choice meaningful to you?

Are you sensing a pattern?

Again, we are not suggesting that you should use one of these prompts as the topic for your 2014 Harvard essay. *But you might.* If you feel that you made a big mistake in your life and learned a lot from it, that absolutely could form the basis for a good essay.

At a minimum, we are presenting this list of questions so you can understand the kind of information that can prove valuable to the adcom in evaluating your application.

As an exercise to help you uncover some potential material for Harvard, we strongly suggest that you go through each of these questions and sketch out your ideas for how you would answer it. You don't have to come up with a unique answer to each version of the "accomplishments" question. But you should be able to answer that question for Harvard – and you might consider using such an answer as part of your 2014 application essay.

Knowing the things you're proudest of – your greatest accomplishments – and understanding some areas of the world you've had exposure to, and, yes, hearing about your career vision – these are all elements that can help the adcom understand a bit about who you are.

Which is the whole point of the application to Harvard or any school.

You need to know who you are before you tackle the Harvard essay. If you're applying to Stanford, it wouldn't hurt to develop your essays for them first – that will force you to do some thinking. (Just please please *please* do not be tempted to re-use Stanford Essay 1 for Harvard's essay. They are NOT the same, and it's so so so completely obvious when someone does this.)

You should probably begin the process of developing your material for Harvard by creating lists. If you list out the things that define you, the experiences that shaped you, the values that you hold, you're going to be identifying the raw material from which your essay can be constructed.

Lists are good. They're a great way to capture your ideas. Knowing what you'd say in response to any of these questions in an interview will serve you well. In fact, EssaySnark predicts that the adcom may turn to some of these questions during their interviews if the applicant didn't cover them sufficiently in the application.

Of course, if you don't cover them sufficiently in the application, you're unlikely to be graced with an interview invite.

Thus, we suggest that these are good areas to explore in your essay.

Provided that you're not sufficiently covering them elsewhere.

Which takes us to this important topic.

What should not be in the Harvard essay

One word: Repetition.

Oh wait. Another word too: TMI.

That is, *too much information.*

Harvard is not typically interested in all the messy personal details of life. If you've been dealing with very difficult problems like depression or family issues like divorce or illness or, even worse, suicide of a relative, we generally discourage you from including these in your HBS essay. They're not generally what Harvard wants to hear about. This is an application to a professional program, remember? If it's something that you wouldn't share in a job interview, then keep it to yourself, and keep it out of your Harvard essay.

The main thing that you should avoid in this essay though? Redundancies.

A Snarky Caveat

The Harvard essay should not be a mere retread of what you're presenting in the other areas of your app.

If your resume is done well, it's going to encapsulate your biggest wins. It's going to give the adcom a lot of information about your career progression and contributions on the job. Your recommenders will also be covering such examples – or they should. You need to coach them to do that. (You can get our Recommender's Instruction Sets product if you want to offer some guidance to your recommenders on literally how they should handle the Harvard recommendation.)

If the two key application assets of *resume* and *recommendations* are doing their job, then you may not need to spend much time, if any, on those parts of your profile in the essay.

Your essay should not be a retelling of the same information that you've got covered elsewhere. In case you didn't notice, that's explicit in the essay prompt.

If your resume is only hinting at some big achievement that deserves to be more fully fleshed out, then sure. You can include the complete story in the essay. That can be a valid strategy.

Just remember that it is possible to submit a Harvard application *with no essay whatsoever.*

Last year, they got 10 applications with no essay. They admitted one. If you didn't believe the adcom's assertions that the essay doesn't carry that much weight, then there's your proof.

Should you skip the essay altogether?

Most people will be uncomfortable with submitting an app with no essay. Most people feel that they need to give the adcom *something*. And that's fine. It would be a courageous BSer indeed who goes forth with applying to Harvard no essay. If you're considering that, we'd encourage you to go through our Sanity Check process to make sure that you're conveying what you need to in the application assets that you've got.

The one situation where we can say almost categorically that it would be unwise to skip the essay is for the BSer who's doing so because they ran out of time.

A strategy of submitting no essay must be *a strategy*. It's not going to work if you came to the party late. If you woke up yesterday and decided to apply to Harvard – and the application is due tomorrow – then you are not going to be successful by submitting it without a full strategy. The no-essay idea must be fully vetted.

We can also say categorically that the only way a no-essay strategy will work is if your resume is superduper awesome.

Most people don't bother with updating their resume before submitting it with their MBA applications. Most people are making a mistake with that. And all people who think that their current look-for-a-job version of the resume is sufficient for Harvard are woefully misinformed.

Everyone needs to create an MBA application resume. It's highly unlikely that you have emphasized the right things in your existing resume. In order to even consider a strategy of not writing the HBS essay, your resume must be dripping with awesome.

That does not mean it should be longer than one page. And it does not mean you can get away with a tiny font to fit it all in. It means that you need to include the most important things and ditch the fluff. It's an art, it is, to write a powerful resume like that.

If you don't want to do the essay for Harvard, make sure your resume is rock solid.

A bigger risk for most people will be in writing *too much*. The open-ended question with unlimited length represents a trap for many people.

Not only do you need to figure out what to write about, but you need to figure out how long to write about it.

What should be *in the Harvard essay?*

Simple: Evidence of your superstar-ness.

(Or rephrased: What should be in the essay is evidence of superstar-ness that cannot be found elsewhere in the app. Or that gives needed detail that appropriately expands on what is found elsewhere. Or that shows how you are an interesting person with unique experiences that will add value to your peers in the Harvard community.)

Snarky Strategy #4

Use your Harvard essay to show how you are Harvard Material.

What does that mean?

You need to include some **examples** of how awesome you are. These need to be stories, little bite-sized chunks of what you did and how you did it and why, that reveal your skills, experiences, interests, and strengths. These stories need to be well thought out and well constructed.

Or, you need to put your storytelling hat on and share how you've had such an unusual life experience, that you will bring a completely unique perspective and interesting viewpoints to the school.

Harvard is *constructing a class.* They are *looking for diversity.* And diversity comes in many forms. There is not one definition for it.

Basically, you need to think like a lawyer. The Harvard essay is a chance for you to make your case for why they should admit you. The essay is one more opportunity for you to demonstrate that you are Harvard Material.

This EssaySnark blahg post applies even though it's talking about career goals essays: http://essaysnark.com/2013/01/career-goals-essays-you-need-to-think-like-a-lawyer/

One HUGE thing you'll be communicating with your Harvard essay is, how do you handle ambiguity? How do you strategize? And, how well do you know yourself? How well do you know Harvard and what they're about?

Yes, you'll be communicating all these things through the way you write the essay – in terms of what you write about, how you structure it, how long you go on with it. Your thought process is revealed through how you handle this assignment. It will be very telling.

If you feel that you need to write pages and pages, then you're misunderstanding the purpose. Remember, Dee Leopold said it's possible to get in *with no essay.*

Anybody can write an essay. Anybody can try to say the right things. The Harvard adcom is more interested in knowing what you have literally *done* in the past – or, perhaps, what your differentiated life experiences have been – than in hearing you harp on and on about how much you want the opportunity to go to Harvard.

In our experience, keeping the focus on the things you've done, rather than the circumstances of your life, is typically a better approach. Just because your parents immigrated to this country with empty pockets and they built a life for their kids here, doesn't mean that YOUR story is actually all that unique. It can be tough to appreciate whether your situation is that unusual compared to the gazillion other candidates who apply. So proceed cautiously if that's the route you decide to take. (This is why it can be so beneficial to work with an admissions consultant – someone who's seen lots and lots of essays. They can be a sounding board for you in determining if your idea is going to help you stand out.)

Also remember to focus on the specifics. It's easy to make claims and grandiose statements in an essay. Don't do that. Instead, shine a light on *who you are* based on the *actions you've taken* and what type of *impact* they have brought.

Again, this is why those previous Harvard essay questions are so valuable.

The best essays tell stories. (Another blahg post: http://essaysnark.com/2012/12/the-really-best-essays-tell-a-story/)

Ideally you'll have two stories in the Harvard essay – maybe three. In very rare occasions, four. These stories will be from the past three to five years. They will be stories that complement each other in some way, that balance each other.

Maybe one story is from work, and another from a big community project. Different angles in each. It's absolutely fine if both stories are from your professional life – that's where HBS tends to place the emphasis – but you should seek for them to offer different aspects about or insights into to your skills and background.

You should be able to cover each story in about 175 to 225 words.

Oh hey: Since you read this far, we wanted to offer you a special deal. We have an essay review service called the Harvard Essay Decimator. Because you purchased this guide and have been diligently studying along, we wanted to reward those efforts with a coupon. Here's $25 if you want to get the HBS essay reviewed:

http://essaysnark.com/coupon/hbs-reader/product/19191/

Must click through this link to purchase. Good only for use by a verified purchaser of this Guide. Please do not share or distribute this coupon code. Services purchased through any unauthorized use will be canceled.

How old can your stories be?

Unlike MIT, there is no rule at Harvard that you must present stories from within the past X number of years – however you if you've been working for at least two years, then it would be better if you didn't go back to college for your essays. This isn't a hard-and-fast rule. If you did something truly dramatic, important and impressive when you were younger, fine, include it if you feel you must (though shouldn't that already be on the resume?).

The problem with that is, since you should not be going on too long with your essay, then you're potentially shortchanging the adcom. They won't get to know who you are TODAY if you use stories that are dated. The Harvard Admissions Board is much more interested in knowing the actions you took and the results you obtained as the person you are now, as an adult, rather than some dated incident that happened during ancient times.

What should your stories be about?

It is perfectly acceptable to have only work-related accomplishments in your Harvard essay. With Harvard, they really care about your professional self. And, they kind of don't care about your personal side – at least, you can definitely get *too* personal in an essay for Harvard. We said that already but it bears repeating: Be careful about TMI with Harvard.

And again: There are no rules. Go in the direction you think is best. But you must be showcasing something that is DISTINCTIVE about yourself. For most people, sticking with the professional domain is safest.

Having a sob story about something traumatic and awful that happened to you is probably not the way to go with this essay. The only possible exception to that is if you're able to present that awful story of difficult circumstances in a way that shows how YOU reacted and behaved when you were faced with it. Then, it could be usable, potentially. But we're doubtful that it's the way to go. You are much more likely to make a strong showing if you focus on your most amazing stories from your career, or possibly one from a community service engagement if you've been involved in a fabulous way with an organization you're passionate about.

If you pull multiple stories from your professional life, make sure they don't all sound the same. For example, maybe you have two stories from two totally separate jobs in different companies. Just because they're from different jobs doesn't mean they're conveying different things about you. Sometimes people use two stories that are really really similar — like a PE guy who talks about independently sourcing and closing a deal, and has a second "failure" or "obstacle" story about making an investment recommendation that went bad. Even if the deals are of two totally different investments in different industries with really different challenges in pulling them together, they're likely going to sound very similar to an adcom reader from the outside. It's important to bring variety to this essay. Either or both of these could be the right stories to present, but you would need to make sure you talk about the different things that you did in each.

In other words, how can you illustrate your strengths and insights and intelligence and contributions to the reader in different ways through the stories you choose? That's your goal — to come through as a well-rounded and unique individual with varied experiences — not as a one-trick pony.

How long should your essay be?

As short as possible. And no more than 800 words. OK, maybe 1,000. But we prefer 800.

Snarky Strategy #5

Be short and sweet in your HBS essay.

In prior years, the HBS adcom allowed 800 words total for BSers to present who they are, in the two essays. We simply cannot imagine a situation where you would need more than that in the single essay they've allowed you this year. You can go up to 1,000 words if you must. That's two double-spaced pages. Which is a lot of writing. What more do you need to say that's not already fully represented on the other application assets you're submitting?

We actually feel that most people should do fine with about 500 words. But we know that most people won't do that.

If you decide to go over 1,000 words, that's your prerogative. EssaySnark is not dictating strategy to you. All we're saying is, that's a very long essay, and please consider it from the perspective of the person who will be reading it on the other end. You'll want to make sure that all of it is necessary. We are skeptical that it truly is.

How to Do It

At risk of stating the obvious, here's the essence of your task with HBS:

1. Figure out what to write about.

2. Figure out how to say it concisely.

Going through the previous HBS essay questions will offer a great exercise in determining your answer to #1. Making your list and checking it twice will help you evaluate what's essay-worthy, and what's not.

Writing an outline of what you (think you) need to say to Harvard will be your key to #2.

Do NOT simply start writing your essay. You need a plan of attack.

This is the tl;dr version of our strategies for the Harvard essay. We actually have a much more involved process which we're going to present subsequently. But for those of you who can't be bothered, then this is what you need to know to structure your material. Hopefully you'll return to this after you've spent time generating ideas for what to say. It'll be much easier for you to structure the material if you have some material to structure!

Structure your ideas

This is what you need to do to start your actual draft:

1. First, write an outline. Get your key points established.

2. Make sure you know directly what the answer to the question is. If the question is, "How well did we get to know you?" then give a straight statement in response. This is your premise.

3. Next, identify your supporting examples. You should have one or maybe two distinct experiences that you're going to share with the Admissions Board in support of your premise.

4. For each example, the focus should be in explaining literally what you did in that situation, and what the outcomes were. Make sure you talk about impact, if relevant. If you're telling a story about how you had a big win at work, for example, then offer enough of an explanation that shows how your contributions were necessary and valued; just don't get too far into the weeds that you lose your reader or bore the pants off of him.

5. Ideally you'll have a reference to the Harvard MBA here somewhere and why it's important to you.

6. Now, write the draft.

7. You may need to go back to re-do the beginning and the ending later. Usually it takes a bit to get the body of your essay established, and then you need to add on an intro and a conclusion that "match" it. Be flexible with how your ideas take shape. The intro sentences that you started out with might not end up being a good fit to how the actual essay developed. Make sure it's all logical and complete in the end.

8. Then obviously PROOFREAD! The best way to catch sneaky little typos is to print it out and read it out loud. Do this more than once, ideally with a significant amount of time (several hours) in between each sitting. Do not rely on spellcheck!

Good luck with it, Brave Supplicant!

Oh. You still don't know what to write? OK, keep reading. But don't forget to come back to this section once you've got the ideas mapped out. The *structure* part of your drafting process is just as important as the *content* of the essay. (Hint: If you're applying to LBS and you get invited to interview, you'll want to use the same technique to develop your on-the-spot presentation.)

A Bunch of Ideas for Generating Ideas

We know, we know. We're giving you a lot of reading to do. Did you think you could just sit down on a Saturday and whip out your essay? It's going to require more work than that.

Here's a series of exercises that you can go through – you may not need all of them, but you will likely find value in completing most.

Take an Inventory

Start with your resume. It encapsulates the bulk of your work experience, right? It's "who you are" in one sense of the word.

What we would suggest is, go through your resume and identify what each bullet point conveys to the reader.

Here's an example:

- Managed $1 million budget, selected vendors, negotiated contracts, and supervised all tenant improvement work for a company-wide move to a larger facility

As a complete stranger reading this, we know these things:

1. The BSer can deal with numbers - "managing a budget" implies that they can work their way around a spreadsheet or other such numbers-crunching tool

2. The BSer is trusted by their organization – a $1M budget is no small potatoes, and if they were the one doing the negotiations, then that's a lot of autonomy

3. The BSer is *probably* a little older – most people new to their careers don't have such responsibilities. Related to this, the BSer *probably* is working for a smaller organization – but not necessarily. Typically though, people of bschool-application-age would not have these responsibilities unless they're at a smaller firm. This is not good nor bad, it's just an observation that can tell us a little something about the BSer's experiences.

Each item on your resume is – or should be!!! – communicating similar things. This is why the essay is not the be-all/end-all for the adcom. They're getting a lot of information already through the other app assets.

The other way to screen your resume: Imagine you're a recruiter – or think back to the job interviews you've had recently. What's the first thing that a hiring manager would want more information on? Do you have any unexplained gaps? Or, are there weird overlaps in dates, because you've been doing side projects, or are working on some type of entrepreneurial venture along with your day job?

Those might be good to list out. They're components of your background that might need to be explained to the Admissions Board.

Now go through the basic stats of your profile – GMAT and GPA particularly. If you're light on quant skills as reflected in those places, then you'll want to boost your profile in the resume and/or the essay to show that you've got the chops for quant. So that might be one place to look for an example to present in the essay.

If your GPA is low, then *maybe* you can include an explanation of why, in the one essay – though we're not so keen on this as a strategy, as it's focusing on a negative, and it's talking about something from a long time ago (probably you graduated at least three years ago), and it would be cheating yourself of an opportunity to talk about something stronger. In fact, that would make for a pretty darn boring essay, most likely. If your grades were *really* bad then you probably do need to take control of your messaging – even better though would be to take a class right now to demonstrate to the adcom that you care about school and can succeed in the classroom. Submitting a transcript for a recent class would speak for itself, you'd not even need to say anything more about it – the adcom would understand what your intentions were. That would then leave you this essay to present something more interesting. It's not out of bounds to talk about college in this essay, though. We probably wouldn't do it but that doesn't mean that you can't. Remember, this is YOUR strategy, not ours.

Go through the stories that you presented in the essays you wrote for the other schools. See what you can deduce about your strengths from what you said there.

Assuming you know what your recommenders are going to talk about, at least generally, then include those stories on your list, too.

What you're doing is **reverse-engineering your profile.** You're examining all the elements that the adcom would examine, and putting them against each other, to see what they communicate – and most importantly, to identify the gaps.

Then, you'll fill those gaps with examples you cite in the essay that demonstrate evidence that the gap is inconsequential, or even better, to turn it into a strength.

Brainstorming

Here's the exact exercise we have our full-engagement clients complete when we start out working together. It's a brainstorming exercise, to get them thinking about their background, their profile, their strengths and weaknesses — and to start generating ideas for essays. You might want to go through this exercise, too (and here's a tip: hang on to the notes that you generate even after you submit your app; you'll want to review them again when you are ready to prep for your interviews):

EssaySnark's brainstorming exercise for new clients

[This is the actual email we send out.]

As another step in developing your application theme, a useful exercise is to brainstorm about your major accomplishments, and your biggest failures. Schools often ask about accomplishments and failures in their essays and interviews, so getting an "inventory" of these, so to speak, will give us a sense of what we can work from in creating your strategy. Put together a simple list of, say, your five (or six, or seven) most important achievements, and two or three of your most spectacular failures.

It's not recommended to write full essays for the purpose of this exercise. People often get attached to a draft if they write it all out; it can be hard to redirect and start over. This exercise is simply about getting some ideas out, not in starting to write the actual essays. If you end up writing a lot, then stop — just capture your key ideas. Make a list, that's all we're looking for. Since this is just for you, a bunch of backstory or explanation is not needed. That can come later, as you flesh the ideas out. For now, you just need to get the gist of it; we shouldn't have to dig through to find the core of the achievement or failure.

These can be taken from literally any area of your life — the classroom, team projects, internships, community engagement with volunteering, extracurriculars from school, sports, even personal things like overcoming illness or dealing with parents' divorce or whatever. Lay it all out on a piece of paper. Anything is fair game at this stage. You need not edit yourself in terms of where these items come from in your life, nor need you worry about how current or ancient history they might be. When you go to create your essays, you'll mostly want to cover what you've done in the past three years or so, but for the purposes of this exercise, you can include anything at all of importance to you. Where were the pivot-points in your life? Where did the track diverge and you started moving in a new direction? These are often tied to achievement or mistake/failure that can be relevant here.

When thinking of accomplishments, try to identify ones where you met a tangible goal ("completed a project two weeks early", "passed an industry exam and received a professional certification", etc.), or specifically, achievements where your efforts made a direct contribution to your team, the customer, or the overall company in ways that can be measured ("reduced costs by 10%", "made the customer so happy that they bought another product from us", etc.).

The best "failure" stories show where there was a lapse in judgment, maybe in trying to cut corners or save time and something got screwed up because of not enough planning. Or a sloppy mistake, like sending out an old version of a dataset, and everyone on the project using the wrong set of numbers, and then everything having to be redone at a lot of expense later on. Or, saying the wrong thing to the wrong person. Anywhere where your exact actions caused problems for others, these can be very good stories to use in essays. This isn't the only angle that the Harvard essay question is asking about, but it can be a useful one to start with.

Here's a video from a few years back by Darden's Director of Admissions with a great idea on how to identify some of these more recent pivotal experiences or moments:

http://youtu.be/dujI_GT6Uxo

Finally, if you're stuck on this: Force yourself to come up with ideas by doing a timed writing exercise. The way it works is this: Set yourself up in a quiet place with a pen and a notepad. This seems to work best done by hand, but you could do it on the computer instead if you wish.

1. At the top of the page, write in big block letters: MY MOST SIGNIFICANT ACCOMPLISHMENTS ARE. (Or, for the second phase, WHERE HAVE I ROYALLY SCREWED SOMETHING UP?)

2. Get a kitchen timer. Set it for five minutes.

3. Put the pen on the paper and start writing — and don't let yourself stop.

Keep that pen moving until the timer goes off. It doesn't matter if you're writing about the topic at first — you could even begin by writing "I have no idea what to write." Just force yourself to write, don't worry about punctuation and spelling, nobody's going to see it. Keep going for the entire five minutes. Don't let the pen stop moving on the page.

Nothing come of it? Give yourself a minute, get a cup of coffee, sit back down and do it again. Maybe change the prompt at the top of the page this time: WHAT AM I MOST PROUD OF? or WHERE HAVE I HAD AN IMPACT ON OTHERS? or WHAT WAS THE BIGGEST MISTAKE I'VE EVER MADE?

You may feel a little silly doing this exercise, but people are often surprised at what comes up — it's a way to force the subconscious mind into action, and sometimes it spits up some real gems!

So that's the first step: Creating a list. Or two, actually.

You can do this exercise a few times – in fact, we're going to ask you to make lists several more times in the next few pages. What you want to do at the beginning of your process is simply to generate ideas. This needs to be unfiltered and uncensored. It's likely that many of your ideas will be crap at first. Give it time and go back to try again. Don't edit them at this phase; just generate them, and see what comes.

One more source for ideas: Harvard's leadership class

Earlier in this guide, we promised to share with you the criteria by which Harvard professors grant grades in the classroom.

We also told you that Harvard looks for evidence that you'll be successful with the case method – which can be a somewhat sharp-elbowed environment. It's not for the faint of heart. The Admissions Board will want to be assured that you can stand up for yourself, that you're assertive, that you will advocate for your own position when you feel the need. (Hint: Any of those topics could make for a great HBS essay.) Expressing an understanding of the case method and/or showing how you're going to be a good contributor in that environment is considered "mission critical" by Dee Leopold (per the July 2014 webinar, in response to a question asked about whether they evaluate people as introverts vs extroverts; she said they do not, but then went on to emphasize that HBS is not for the meek).

To help you better understand literally what the professors go on in evaluating their students, here's the guidelines for grading from a core leadership class – and these questions could make for a great starting point for some further brainstorming on your behalf.

Your grade will be based on class participation and on the final exam. Your professor will inform you of how these components will be weighted in class. With regard to participation, quality is weighted more than quantity. Quality includes, among other things:

1. impact on peers' thinking;

2. sound, rigorous, and insightful diagnosis (e.g., sharpening of key issues, depth and relevance of analysis);

3. realistic and effective action recommendations;

4. constructive critiques of others' contributions;

5. integrative comments (across cases and/or courses);

6. so called "stupid questions" that no one else is willing to take the risk to ask;

7. clarity and conciseness of presentation; and

8. evidence of active listening (e.g., relevance and timing of comments).

The first three are especially rich.

Can you think of a time when you were especially persuasive, and your ideas had an impact on others' thinking? How about a time when you uncovered the root cause of a problem that escaped everyone else? What about an example of coming up with a solution that turned out to be ideal?

All of these could be useful for your recommenders to consider as well, particularly #6. You might want to share this with them when you meet to discuss what they would say about you in the letter that they write.

We're emphasizing these questions, and the experience of the case method in general, because it's long been the hallmark of business school education at Harvard.

Here's a quote from a Harvard student who felt that he was finally able to synthesize what the case method is about:

After reading what feels like hundreds of cases already, I think I've also finally realized what the case method aims to do. It's about teaching people how to constantly listen and connect the dialog into a single stream conclusion. Obvious perhaps, but also far harder to do than it sounds. I've caught myself suffering from delayed-response syndrome a few times, where the pieces don't quite fit until a couple minutes later, by which time the conversation may have moved on. Despite that, I'm enjoying the experience, and know that it will be vital for an introvert like me to slowly build up confidence to put my (even half-baked) thoughts forward.

That's from this blog:

http://hbsrecruiting.wordpress.com/2014/01/09/looking-back-on-1st-semester-and-looking-forward-to-2nd-semester/

The case method in the classroom means you have to have the intellectual horsepower, and the self-confidence, to keep up. Have you been in a high-stakes environment where you've been put on the spot to add value? Might be something to talk about in your Harvard essay.

Harvard Essay Ideas: An Accomplishment

So you've got your lists, and you've evaluated the different stories against each other to see which ones might offer unique insights in different ways. How do you go about presenting the actual "something you did well"?

As we've been hammering home, you need to be clear on what you want the adcom to know about you. You want them to see a balanced picture. You want to show them multiple sides of yourself, your accomplishments from different parts of your life. And, obviously, you want this accomplishment to be IMPORTANT.

You could pretend that the essay question is more like the ones they asked for the past umpteen years:

> **What are your three most substantial accomplishments and why do you view them as such?**

In other words, EssaySnark predicts that your best Harvard essay will come out if you think of this as writing about your MOST SIGNIFICANT ACCOMPLISHMENTS. If you can include an awareness of that "why significant" angle, then it will help inform your writing in a powerful way.

This is a non-trivial task! Just selecting the right accomplishment is fraught with challenges. Then, figuring out *how to present it* – and then layering in the very sophisticated angle of why you think it's significant – all of this will require multiple drafts. You are unlikely to get this down in just one sitting. You should plan to write and rewrite these examples.

So the story you choose to tell should not just be "something" you've done well. It should be your *most significant something*. It should be the one thing – maybe two – that means the most to you. To go out on a limb: It maybe even should be the one thing you've ever done that most radically changed your life.

Why don't you jot down the one most majorest achievement or biggest big win or the most impressive personal accomplishment that you've done, that could fit in this category? Maybe you already captured this on your brainstorming list – but maybe not.

My single most significant accomplishment is:

_____

_____

_____

_____

Here's an imprecise and inexact broad-strokes recommendation of what accomplishment to select for inclusive in the Harvard essay:

1. One approach is for this essay to feature your absolute best, biggest, most impressive, most impactful **career-related achievement**(s)

2. Or, potentially, you could talk about an accomplishment that showcases how you've **contributed to a community** (volunteering, nonprofit, etc.) – this would need to be a pretty big over-the-top, definitely not plain-vanilla, type thing. This cannot be just a fundraiser that you contributed to, or a charity 5K that you raised money for. This can't be how you coordinated your sorority's rush during senior year (unless you're a 2+2 candidate, and then sure). This would need to be on a different playing field than those quite typical activities. In fact, instead of one like that, we'd prefer to see you talk about a second professional achievement.

3. Or, potentially, this could be a big personal accomplishment, maybe something with team sports, or music, or overcoming a personal challenge such as significant weight loss.

The main litmus test for whichever accomplishment(s) you choose: It **needs to be something that you personally took action to achieve.** It could be fine and great if it is a team-based achievement, either sports or on the job or whatever, but if so, it needs to be directly YOUR accomplishment, that you worked towards, that you pulled off. It can't be something where you were just along for the ride. Your input into the outcome needs to be primary.

One of the core attributes for an accomplishment is that there is impact on somebody – you or somebody else. You'll need to do several things if using it in the Harvard essay:

1. **Clearly define the accomplishment.** This needs to come through in the first few sentences; the reader should not have to hunt around to know what you're going to present in answer to the question. Clear and succinct are critical here.

2. **Directly explain, with details, what you did to achieve this thing.** The focus needs to be on your actions – in a way that hopefully gives insights into who you are. Based on what you describe for how you achieved it, the reader should be able to glean information about you such as your skillsets, your level of motivation, your ingenuity and creativity, etc. These are things that we read between the lines when we go through a piece of personal writing, and these are all fundamental to making this particular essay work in the strongest way possible. Remember, they're asking about what you *did well.* The emphasis needs to thus be on what you did. Don't overlook this very important aspect!

3. **Provide an indication of impact.** So you did all these things and it resulted in X – OK great, so what? How did that affect others? How did it affect you? If you can include a statement or two along these lines, it will elevate the significance of the story naturally, and it will help the reader see *how you are a leader.* Impact is a measure of leadership. Make sure you touch on that here.

4. **Give a hint as to why you see it as significant.** This may be self-evident from the achievement itself, which is great. Or, perhaps you can fit in an explanation in the opening or closing paragraph about why you chose this to present, or what its meaning is to you, that might be a nice touch too. Ideally though, it should be obvious to any reader why this is an important thing.

If you're looking to make this an even more tightly targeted pitch, you might also try to tie your accomplishment back to your career goals somehow. This could work as a takeaway message in the conclusion, something along the lines of "because I had this experience, I gained this and learned that, and this has set me up to pursue the goals of being a whoop-di-whoop after I graduate from Harvard." This sometimes comes across as smarmy, so you'll need to handle it carefully if you decide to try it.

Please avoid these clichéd topics

Running a marathon does not qualify for this essay. Lots and lots of people talk about running marathons. You might still be able to make it work, but we're skeptical. Just be aware of how often the adcom will have read the exact-same essay. Unless you did it at Boston and you went from the finish line to helping rescue victims in a triage unit – and you then raised $50,000 to help the survivors through your own fundraising efforts afterwards, then we're not convinced it's Harvard essay worthy. To make it more impactful for the reader, you must show how it had an impact on YOU. If you have run one or multiple marathons, we'd be inclined to suggest that you put them at the bottom of the resume and leave it at that.

The other very typical topic in bschool essays is travel. It comes up often in Harvard essays, yet it shouldn't. Travel is not an accomplishment; having gotten on lots of airplanes and having had your passport stamped in multiple places does not show us what type of person you are.

Yes, international experiences are useful for the adcom to know about, as we discussed earlier, but this needs to be more than just the fact that you're well-traveled. You would be surprised how many bschool applicants have been to 10+ different countries. Again, this is still a subject you could potentially explore, but it's tricky. You'd need to integrate it into your theme to make it 'pop.' Maybe you can pull out one specific from the experience and zoom in on it, to explain how it affected you, and why it's important. International experiences are important in a bschool application, however they can also be pretty boring for the adcom to read. The best stories show how the experience changed you.

Yes, the adcom wants to know about you, but just with the other essays, they want to know about you *in relation to the world.* How have you had an impact on others? Or, how has the world had an impact on you? What have been the pivot points in your life? A story describing this — with the focus on WHAT YOU DID — can definitely make for a good essay topic.

Another cliché: **Don't go on about how important family is to you.** Family is important to everyone. You *might* be able to get away with that for Stanford essay 1 but we strongly discourage this as a topic for Harvard.

You should also avoid gimmicks like using a quote from a famous person to lead off — unless you know that famous person personally — or talking about how your grandfather worked hard and inspired you.

This essay must be about YOU. You need to offer the adcom new information that helps them understand you as a unique, interesting, multifaceted and accomplished individual who will add texture to their incoming class.

Harvard Essay Ideas: Talking About a Failure

As you noted from the past years' questions, Harvard has frequently asked applicants to write essays on a time when things didn't work out. When they did something poorly. Many years back they asked about a failure, at other times they asked about a mistake, and last year they wanted to hear about setbacks and things that didn't go well.

This indicates that these are possible areas to explore as you evaluate your potential essay material. That last term is especially helpful here: the word "setback" implies something of a "temporary" nature — a problem or hurdle *that you subsequently overcame.* If you have something in that category, that's significant enough, it can be a good template to use. Think about something that you didn't do well at, but that you eventually turned into a success.

Maybe you're remembering an occasion where everything went sideways. A spectacular failure. That might be a good topic — as long as it is a situation you eventually took action to resolve. In most cases, you'll want a happy ending on the story. You should have a way to show how you grew and learned and became a better person from this experience, where you redeemed yourself somehow. It would be good to illustrate how you did not repeat the same mistake when faced with another such situation in a future time. Don't end your example on a downer note of everything falling apart and that's it. Show the reader how you turned your failure to a positive.

Since Harvard wants to see evidence of where you've been an achiever, then an ideal subject could be an area that doesn't come quite so naturally to you — where you've had to work harder to be a success.

As we stated earlier, Harvard previously asked a question something like this:

> ### *What have you learned from a mistake?*

It wouldn't hurt to treat this year's essay as an opportunity to talk about that if you can. Typically the most interesting essays to read for this type of question are ones where the candidate royally screwed something up and had to fix it. It's very refreshing, and often a little entertaining, to read stories about where someone created some problems for themselves, and to see what they did to recover from it.

What are you currently thinking might work as the topic for this essay? Make note of your ideas.

My biggest setbacks, failures, and mistakes have been when:

_____

_____

_____

_____

_____

If you were dealing with a sick relative who you had to go home regularly to care for during college, for example, that's totally worth mentioning in this essay. Or if you worked 20+ hours a week during school.

Note that the best stories for both of these Harvard topics will identify a goal that you were working towards, and then will discuss what you literally did to try to achieve that goal, and what happened as a result of your actions. As we've been saying repeatedly, it's the *specifics* that will make your essay stand out from the others.

This isn't a rule, but personally, we would avoid using stories from childhood — unless they are truly remarkable or they somehow shed light on who you are now. An extreme example: we once had a client who was homeless as a child — this definitely shaped who she is today.

You could potentially use this essay to discuss overcoming personal obstacles like beating cancer, recovering from a car accident, bouncing back from being laid off during the economic crisis, etc — as long as we can see what you did to get through it. And remember, as mentioned before, HBS typically has a preference for more hardcore professional stories, rather than warm-fuzzy personal ones. This is an application to *business* school, after all. If it's not a story you would volunteer in the middle of an interview for an important new job, then it's probably not one that the Harvard Admissions Board needs to know about, either.

Another bit of advice that may be relevant for some of you as you start to piece together some ideas: No whining.

People have many definitions of "leader" but for sure, "whining and complaining" does not fit in anyone's. Do not paint yourself as a victim in your essay! Do not talk about bad stuff that happened and how you were defeated by it. You need to show how you rose above, how you met the challenge, how you kept going in the face of the obstacle, how you persevered and succeeded. People sometimes make the mistake of talking about bad stuff that other people did *to* them. This is rarely a good presentation. It leaves a negative taste in the mouth. It does not make you sound like a hero. So even if your boss was a real jerk and everyone else was to blame for how the project got all effed up, reposition it in the telling! You need your essays to be factual, but you can always spin them to the positive.

A Snarky Caveat

Be careful about unintended messages.

If you want to explain some hiccups on your resume and you write an essay about how you were laid off during the economic downturn, not just once, not twice, but you were laid off three separate times — you should take a real hard look at that. Are you inadvertently telling the adcom that you're damaged goods? Sure, people get laid off all the time and it doesn't mean that they're losers. And lots of people were laid off during the economic crisis. That alone will not be held against you. But to say that it happened to you *three times* could be raising a red flag.

And the other problem is, what can you show to the reader about who you are, based on how you handled it? You were laid off three times, and then what? You went out and got a new job. There's not typically a lot to be gleaned from that. It's what anyone would do.

Be sure that you're not accidentally telling the adcom that you're a loser, based on what you choose to present. This is why, if you choose to include a "failure" or "obstacle" story in your essay, that it's stronger to write about *mistakes that you made* — problems that you personally caused — rather than stuff that just "happened" to you.

Before you start writing the essays — step back and ask yourself, *What do I want the takeaway message to be?*

What are you trying to communicate about yourself with these examples from your life?

It's likely that all the accomplishments that you've identified through the brainstorming that you've done are valid and important. You can possibly suggest that one or more of your recommenders cover one or more of them in their write-ups. And, obviously, the resume can communicate many of them. It's up to you to identify which ones are the right ones to write about in the essay, and which can be relegated to other parts of your strategy. You need to insert the information where it fits best.

Back to your choice of topics:

You'll need to look at the messaging you're creating. What do you want the adcom to know about you as a result of this combination of stories?

You should be able to extract a specific word or two about each one, a couple of adjectives that are the key ideas of the stories. Add them up. Are these qualities that you think make you into a Harvard MBA candidate?

If someone knows just these few stories about you, what is the net-net? What do you think a complete stranger would assume to be true about the type of person you are, based on just those example?

Now look at your answer to the career goals question in the online application (which you should have written already before getting this far on the essay).

Do the takeaway messages of these specific examples support your pitch of why you want an MBA? And why you *deserve* to be at Harvard Business School, based on what you've done and the kind of person you are?

You may need to tweak it a little — or a lot — before you find the right combination.

While you go through the process of thinking up ideas and evaluating them and scratching them off the list – don't scratch any off the list permanently.

Snarky Strategy #6

Keep building this list of your key accomplishments, strengths, and qualities. You may need it later.

If you are indeed "Harvard material" then you will find yourself coming up with plenty of possible essay topics as you struggle with what to present. It is not an easy task to identify which are the strongest. But don't worry about it too much, because even if you can't fit an important story into your essay, and even if your references to it on your resume and the application dataset seem too abbreviated to convey its importance, and even if you can't get one of your recommenders to talk about it – you still may have a chance to present it to the Admissions Board later. That's because they're offering up a final opportunity for candidates to add to the pitch following the interview. See a discussion on this later in this *Guide*. For now, you should be capturing your ideas on paper, and not discarding them. Maintain a running list. You never know how you may need that later on.

OK, onwards (we're almost done!).

So what's a good reason to want to go to Harvard?

Because that's what HBS is asking with that application question "How does pursuing an MBA support your [Intended Post-MBA career] choices?"

Unfortunately there are SO MANY PEOPLE who do not have any reason at all for wanting to go to this school. They often hardly know why they want an MBA. Mostly these people are caught up in the *idea* of a Harvard MBA. It's the prestige factor. Harvard is the movie star of MBA programs, and they just want to be associated with its glamor. Or their dad wants them to go to Harvard. They haven't put much more thought into it than that.

These people rarely get in.

You need to at least tell the adcom why you want the MBA in terms of directionally how it will get you where you are saying you want to go.

Yes it's tough to even narrow down your career interest into the options offered in those Industry and Function dropdown boxes. But this is an important process to go through. (Again, you may decide to tackle another school's formal career goals essay before trying to identify the industry and function for Harvard – the thinking you'll be forced to do to craft that other essay will help you in figuring out what to select here.)

Basically what Harvard is asking for in 500 small characters is for you to tell them directly why an MBA is important to your plans.

Fair enough. You're saying you want one, here's your chance to say why.

Focus your answer on (you guessed it) SPECIFICS if you can – and write it in the context of why you want to go to *Harvard,* not just why you want to go to any ol' bschool. Focus on the actual skills and training that you need. Do a gap analysis: Take your stated target industry and function as a starting point, and work backwards. Why can't you go get that job right now? Besides the advantage of Harvard Career Services and recruiting help, what literally are you looking to gain from the experience of going to this school?

Recognize also that the "why" question is much more than just the fact that going to Harvard will enable your career goals. The career goal is encapsulated in your choices in the two dropdown menus above. If you have personal reasons ("my fiancé is currently attending the Kennedy School" or "my father went to HBS") then those possibly could be mentioned here, though with such limited space, you're going to need to err on the side of your own specific reasons and the actual aspects to Harvard that appeal to you.

This is where your on-the-ground research will pay off the most. You need to beat feet and:

- Visit campus.

- Talk with current students.

- Reach out to all the HBS alumni that you can get your hands on.

You need to be able to answer the question: What is unique and different about this school?

(There's at least ONE REALLY BIG THING that you should definitely be talking about here — and sorry, we're not going to write this answer for you. You should be able to figure out how HBS does things differently and what's the important stuff that's worth mentioning. Because after all, you're HBS material, are you not??)

The timeframe for this answer can also include your longer-term target. The answers you choose in the dropdown menus should obviously be focused on what you will do straight out of school, immediately after you graduate. It's fair to then mention a longer-term interest in the short answer, but you don't need too much in this area. If HBS wanted to know about your long-term goal, then they would have literally asked you about it. So a directional target is fine though we usually prefer to see a little more specificity, as we've said.

A few more comments:

- If you're looking to use Harvard to make some **radical career change**, you should try to touch on what your new direction looks like, and how you're qualified to pursue it (the resume will need to work to back you up on this part). As "transformative" an education as the HBS MBA may be, it's not enough on its own to help someone go from one very different career in a whole new direction. Your short answer should be an obvious and natural statement for someone who's presented themselves as a particular type of person already through the essay and on the resume and through the recommendations. These elements should all be working together to paint a picture of someone who can "transform" into the direction you're defining here in this answer. You need to show the adcom that you have transferable skills and are equipped to make the transition to the new field.

    This can be especially critical for those going in a very dissimilar direction, e.g., IT guys wanting to go into finance. You'll need to show how you're ready to make this leap.

- Conversely, if you're not showing ENOUGH transition — if your stated **short-term goal is too similar** (or even identical) to what you are already currently doing in your job today — then you're not giving the adcom enough evidence of why you need a high-powered HBS MBA. You should position yourself as ADVANCING, and then show how the MBA is the one main requirement that you need to get from A to B.

- You do not necessarily have to talk about saving the world — and in fact, if you have not done much "save the world" stuff in the past (like, if you have never volunteered a day in your life), then you should probably either start volunteering fast, or figure out a different "why do I want to go to Harvard" answer than that. Everything needs to be consistent. All the pieces need to add up.

So you've got a handle on that? Good. How about you take a crack at defining your "post-MBA professional goals" next?

What do you want to do immediately upon graduation from HBS?

_____

_____

_____

You'll want to refine this. And also practice it as part of your elevator pitch. You'll need it in interviews, too. But three lines should be plenty enough to capture the gist of it here.

Now how about this one: **Why do you need an MBA in order to accomplish that?**

_____

_____

_____

_____

Here's another very valid exercise to go through: **Why do you specifically need to go to Harvard to achieve this?**

_____

_____

_____

_____

So many candidates simply get all goo-goo about Harvard. *Everybody* wants to go to Harvard. To be compelling in your essays, you'll need to explain *why* you want to go there — why *you personally* want to.

This is where you need to go beyond what you've read on the website (though that information could be relevant). This is where you want to apply what you know about HBS, from all the research you've done — you have visited the school, right? — and shown how you understand what the school is about and why you need the advantage that they can offer in pursuing your ambitions.

Evaluate your ideas

Before committing an idea to paper, you need to make sure that it's adding value for you.

Here's a checklist:

- Is everything you want to say being presented as a CONCRETE, TANGIBLE example?

- What is your POINT in presenting each item that you want to present? What's the intended TAKEAWAY MESSAGE? What qualities or attributes does each item convey?

- Does each example capture NEW INFORMATION about who you are — info that's not already conveyed elsewhere in your app assets?

- Is that new information CRITICAL to who you are?

- Validate it: What would be the impact if you DID NOT include this story? Would the reader miss out on understanding something imperative about you and your background?

- Finally: Does this example give the adcom evidence of you as a leader? Or, does it show how you've had especially unusual or unique experiences that will allow you to contribute to the school community?

Remember: Leadership can be conveyed in many many ways, and not every single item you include in your essay needs to be explicitly presenting leadership qualities per se. But most of them should. Just don't get black-and-white on this. Leadership is a malleable, flexible term. It means a lot of things. You can demonstrate important leadership characteristics in a variety of ways. We're not suggesting that if a story you want to include doesn't squarely hit some predefined idea of "leadership", that you should ax it. We are suggesting that most of your stories should add up to presenting the adcom with evidence of this "habit of leadership" which they are looking for.

As you go through possible stories to include, you should always be reflecting back on your overall platform. What exactly are you communicating through your choice of these specific stories? What do you want the adcom to think of you after they go through your essays? You are the one who gets to control that impression. based on what you choose to present to them in the first place.

Finally: You do not need to tell the full story of every little nook and cranny of your background in the essay. If it's on your resume and is being depicted clearly enough there, then that will suffice for all manner of things that the adcom needs to know about. Your job with the essay, as part of the full set of materials being submitted with your application, is to get the adcom interested enough in you that they want to meet you for an interview. Trust the process.

So that's that. Now you have everything you need to tackle the application strategy for Harvard Business School, in order to "introduce yourself" (as they put it) to the Admissions Board.

FAQs on the Harvard Application

We've gotten a few questions from Brave Supplicants on aspects on the online application to Harvard Business School that we decided to share with you. Please note that when we developed this 2014 application guide, the application hadn't been released yet, so these may or may not map to literally what the school asks at the time you fill it out (though it should be directionally accurate).

1. *For the HBS application under the Employer section, how should I answer the Most Significant Challenge (200 characters)? Do I only describe the challenge? Do I describe the challenge and my actions/result against that challenge? Should I align the challenge with something my recommenders will speak to?*

   ANSWER: The significant challenge for HBS should be as fully-formed as you can make it; it may or may not also be touched on in the essay (or by a recommender) but there are no strict rules. The challenge itself should be clear, and it should hopefully be something that you successfully overcame, but the important part is WHAT it was. The severity or complexity or sophistication of what you were facing in that role will give the adcom many insights into role itself.

   Our main warning to you is: Don't overthink this!! It's important for the reader to instantly grasp whatever it is that you define as the "challenge" – so nothing overly complicated. But don't feel limited, it can be from across the spectrum of experiences of a job – technical, interpersonal, political, etc (just be careful if going down the latter path).

2. *How should I answer the Key Accomplishments (200 characters)? Should the accomplishments I list differ from those on my resume? Should they add detail to the resume accomplishments?*

   ANSWER: If something qualifies as a "key accomplishment" for the purpose of reporting it that way in the application, then it definitely belongs on the resume – and it *might* be worthy of discussion in the essay too (though again, be careful about not repeating yourself, as we warned at the beginning of this guide). We've seen people write these application answers in full sentences, and others do them as phrases or sentence fragments. The way you handle it is up to you. No matter what, 200 characters is not much!

3. *What do I put down for AWA if I just took my GMAT and don't have the score yet?*

   ANSWER: Enter "0.0" if you don't have the AWA score. You must have a GMAT or GRE score to apply but you don't need to have the AWA component reported when you submit the app if it's not available yet.

4. ***The deadline is tomorrow and one of my recommenders hasn't submitted yet!***

   ANSWER: It's OK; HBS admissions gives recommenders a little extra time. Just make sure that the recommendation is submitted in the next day or so and you'll be fine.

5. ***I'm a reapplicant. Are they going to look at last year's app?***

   ANSWER: Not initially, no. They'll make the decision on whether to invite you to interview without looking at your previous submission. Once you've been invited, then the Admissions Board person who will be doing your interview will pull up everything from last year. For that reason, you will want to most definitely vary the topic that you covered on the essay. As Dee Leopold said in the July 2014 webinar, "If you're talking about the same general topic, then at least put a different reflection on it. You don't want to give impression that all you did was a copy-and-paste from last year." Don't submit the same pitch and expect it to work out differently. Bring some insight into your candidacy today.

6. ***If I applied through 2+2 originally, am I a reapplicant if I apply again now?***

   ANSWER: Yes.

Finally, this last bit isn't about the app or admissions, but just something you should know about Harvard:

The first year is the Required Curriculum, referred to as "RC", and first-year students are called "RCs". The second year is the Elective Curriculum, or "EC", and second-years are called "ECs". If you want to get a sense for the difference between the two contingents of students, then this video is helpful:

http://youtu.be/xR8CNTbYXoE

OK, moving on...

The Harvard Interview

We actually cover a good deal of information and guide you on prep for interviews in the *EssaySnark Interviewing Guide*, however the Harvard interview process is stressful enough, and different enough, that we'll touch on some of the essential elements here.

Interviews are mandatory at Harvard before anyone is accepted. The way the process works is that several weeks after the round deadline, HBS will begin issuing interview invitations, usually in batches (though this year, we have the suspicion that they may opt to do just one "interview invite day" where they invite everyone and be done with it – we think that could be why they pulled the deadline up further in September than it was before). We don't have information on any changes yet though so we'll just talk about how they've done things in the past.

They typically do one batch of invites on two Wednesdays in a row. In the second batch, they will also "release" any candidates who they have decided to take a pass on. That mid-cycle release date will be announced on Dee Leopold's blog after the respective round deadline has passed. You could potentially be placed straight on the waitlist on that "release" day, without going through an interview first – they call this the "Further Consideration" list. If you're in that limbo, you could potentially get an interview invite in Round 2. There is no "Further Consideration" in Round 2; instead, if they like you some but not quite enough, you would be placed directly on the waitlist after an interview, or released.

On an interview invite day, all of that day's invites will come out in a batch via email, typically right around noon Eastern time. You'll be hovering over your inbox at that time. If you don't have your invite by a few minutes after 12:00pm, then that means you're not getting one that day.

A few days after that first batch of invites go out, they'll open up the interview scheduling system; this usually happens on the Friday or the Monday after the invitations are issued.

Then it's a free-for-all: everyone gets to select their own interview slot, either in Cambridge, or Silicon Valley, or a few international locations, e.g., London and Dubai and somewhere in South America, and sometimes (not always) in Delhi or Mumbai. The appointments go fast, so if you're in the first batch of invites, then you'll want to log onto the scheduling site ASAP when it goes live; if you're in a later batch, you need to schedule right away when you get the invite. They don't open additional slots with each new batch of invites, so if you're invited at the end, there will be fewer to choose from, though Harvard admissions promises that no one is ever left out in the cold due to scheduling problems. They *will* find a way to interview you, if you've received an invitation to do so.

Keep in mind that there is literally *nothing* to be interpreted from when Harvard issued your interview invite. The people who are invited in the first batch are not necessarily the strongest candidates; it's not that they like them the best. Instead it's just a factor of their review cycles and how long it takes to get through the batch of apps. Don't try to interpret anything; there are no tea leaves to be read here. It has nothing to do with when you submitted your application – back in June, or on deadline day, both are evaluated in exactly the same way. It has nothing to do with your geography – Australia and Hawaii and everyone in between are all handled the same. People get themselves so psyched out about such insignificant things. This is one datapoint — when the invite comes — that is meaningless.

The one thing that's true: It's more likely you'll get an invitation on the first day of invites, if you're going to get one at all, only because they issue the vast majority of them then. (This is another reason why there's a possibility that they'll be consolidating everything to a single-day system this year. They already have the bulk of the apps evaluated by the first date, why not just allow a little extra time and evaluate them all?)

What is massively more meaningful is the fact that you got invited to interview at all. Harvard interviews about 1,800 or 1,900 candidates, assuming they will be accepting about 1,100. For the 2013 season, they interviewed 1,887 out of 9,543, which turns out to be just under 20% of all applicants; there are about 940 students in the Class of 2016.

Their numbers are consistent year to year; they don't interview more candidates just because they receive more applications. This is because their yield (the number of offers they extend which are accepted by people who actually enroll) is very stable, and it's very high. It's been at 89% for years. So they have predictable numbers going through this part of the cycle.

They interview enough candidates such that you would have about a 50/50 chance of acceptance at that stage. That's obviously hugely better than the 12% acceptance rate for the overall pool. Getting to the interview stage is obviously a very good sign.

The main reason most candidates blow it at the interview are when their essay doesn't match up to how they present in person (i.e., someone else wrote the essay), and/or they come across as arrogant.

The interview counts for a lot. In fact, Harvard claims that the "extensive interview process" is a main reason why they are able to cut back on the essay question requirements. They don't need the written application to make their final determination. They're going to meet you in person to do that.

It's OK to be nervous for your interview — in fact, it's to be expected. The best way to minimize the jitters is to do plenty of prep work ahead of time (again, you can check out the EssaySnark blahg for help on interview prep).

For Rounds 1 and 2, the Admissions Board travels to specific cities around the world to conduct interviews, or you can travel to Cambridge and interview on campus. If you can pull that trip off, you should do so. It's worth it to be in the middle of all the action for the interview, and it shows that you are motivated and dedicated to the school. It doesn't hurt you if you can't do it, but it can only help you if you can.

Note that sometimes HBS does not travel to India for interviews, which seems to make people quite upset. There were rumblings one year that HBS was discriminating somehow by not doing so. Not quite sure how that logic works, since Indian candidates were invited to interview, they just had to travel to Dubai in meet the adcom.

The Admissions Board does not travel for Round 3 candidates; if you apply in the last round, you must go to Cambridge for the interview.

In unusual circumstances, the Admissions Board will conduct an interview via Skype, though this is reserved for extreme cases, such as candidates in the military on active deployment. If you're applying to Harvard, you should start planning now for how you'll make yourself available at one of their interview destinations at your own expense when the time comes.

Yes, it might be expensive and it might be inconvenient. Most everything about bschool is both expensive and inconvenient. This is a massive investment in *you*; if you can't be bothered to make the interview happen based on the Admissions Board's processes, then maybe this whole idea isn't the best one for you.

And in case you're worried about the scheduling: There should be plenty of time between when you get the interview invitation, and when you have to have the interview completed. It should be very feasible to get a plane ticket and secure some vacation time from work or whatever you have to do to get yourself there. This won't be something like you get an email on it today and the interview needs to be done at the end of next week. Timeframes are more abbreviated for a Round 3 interview invite, but even then it's reasonable. The Admissions Board knows that you are busy, that you have a life, that arrangements will need to be made. It's not difficult to make it happen under the parameters they lay out.

As mentioned, interviews at Harvard are always invitation-only, and they are conducted by members of the Admissions Board themselves. This is different than how it works at many schools, where the adcoms tend to recruit the alumni and current students to do the bulk of the interviewing. Harvard doesn't do it that way. Harvard's adcom are very experienced and they are very aware of exactly what it is they're looking for in a candidate – thus, they keep tight control over the process. They feel (and EssaySnark tends to agree) that the best way to get a sense of the applicants is to have the same small set of people have these interactions with those applicants. At some schools, the interview is very unpredictable. We've heard of plenty of occasions where the candidate had a negative experience, and where the report provided by the interviewer undoubtedly was not fair. Harvard avoids all these problems. They have a better system for quality control and consistency. They have a much better sense of who they are admitting than another school can, just based on the fact that it's this small team making the decisions after actually meeting with the candidates themselves.

One word of caution: Sometimes the Harvard interview experience consists of the main Admissions Board interview, plus an observer in the room with you who takes notes. We tell you this just so that you can be prepared for the possibility, as we've heard that it has thrown people at times. If you end up in this situation, then you should direct your answers primarily to the person who's actually interviewing you, but don't be afraid to look at the note-taker and smile once in awhile. Don't pretend that he or she is invisible. Be sure to thank that person at the end, as well.

The main difference with a Harvard interview as opposed to most other schools is that it's an open interview. The person you meet with will have read your entire application and will have questions prepared for you that are specific to you. These cannot be predicted in a vacuum (though EssaySnark can help you prep for this experience if you'd like some guidance; see the website for options). You can expect the Harvard interviewer to have completely read your resume, gone to the website of your employer and any charity you're involved with, and possibly even looked up information on any Harvard alumni who wrote a recommendation for you. They will have done their research before showing up for the interview, and you should do so, too.

What that means for your part is that you need to re-read your essay several times before the interview – believe it or not, you will have forgotten what you wrote about by the time the invite comes along. You need to analyze your own career goals and see if you can find any holes in your aspirations, any obvious gotchas or things that don't make sense (obviously we hope that there aren't any truly obvious things like this – and if there are you likely won't have the privilege of going to interview – but you should go through this analysis process nonetheless). You should hang on to your notes from the brainstorming exercises that you completed, and review all of them again when it comes time to interview.

At a minimum, ask your friend to go through your essays and ask you questions about them.

- "Why" questions are good:"Why did you make that decision?" or "Why didn't you consider this other option?"

- "How" questions are also good: "How did you accomplish that?" or "How did they react when you did that?"

You also need to practice answering questions like why do you want to go to Harvard, etc. Again, we wrote a whole book on how to prepare for the MBA interview, so you may want to pick that up to guide your process.

The Post-Interview Reflection

This is another unique aspect to the Harvard application. They call this step "Have the last word" and its purpose is twofold:

1. Candidates often leave the interview and instantly panic, realizing that they forgot to mention *this one thing*, or feeling like they totally bombed it on *this other thing*. There is significant angst after any interview, the Harvard interview especially. Most people report that it went poorly – even those who end up making it in. Many candidates feel like they left the application process on a weak note. The Post-Interview Reflection gives them a chance to fix this. It alleviates much of that applicant angst.

2. Of course, this step creates a whole new set of angst: You have to complete it quickly. Which probably means, without any input from anyone. Which of course is the adcom's obvious intent. The Post-Interview Reflection must be submitted within 24 hours of the interview. For most people, this means they'll be developing this puppy completely on their own; it's less likely that any admissions consultant who helped with their application will be able to offer much input, given the tight turnarounds.

   In fact, Harvard offers up a study room on campus for applicants to complete their write-up. You can go from your interview straight to your laptop and type out your answer on the spot. It's what the adcom is hoping for. Our advice? We suggest you sleep on it, and rewrite it again, and definitely proofread it carefully – don't just whip it out in the first 20 minutes after the interview and call it a day – it's definitely more important than that.

Dee Leopold stated that one reason for this process is because it mimics the real world: in your future career, there will likely be many occasions when your boss asks you to write up a report and have it on her desk in the morning. So it's a true-to-life exercise that will help the Admissions Board evaluate your capabilities in a more realistic (or at least, less artificial) setting. That's also a reason she offered when announcing the single-essay application last year. It's closer to the Real World.

What does the Post-Interview Reflection consist of?

As of this writing [May 2014], we can't say for sure what this year's version will be, but we can report on what applicants were assigned previously. They were asked to write about a question that is remarkably similar to the main essay question itself:

You've just had your HBS interview. Tell us about it.
How well did we get to know you?

With that type of prompt, then you obviously need to know in advance who you are and what you've been trying to communicate to the Admissions Board. You will want to have a handle on what your theme is, and what backup evidence you can offer to support that theme. All of these elements, you will notice, are the main focus in the exercises we have laid out for you here.

If you have diligently gone through the work in this book and spent time with each step, and gone back over the exercises and re-examined your answers, you should have plenty of raw material from which to construct an answer to this question.

Just like with the essay, this is an opportunity for you to showcase your ability to think. You can demonstrate how you tackle a thought exercise, and how you structure your ideas.

A Snarky Caveat

Just like with the essay, we would caution you:

Don't repeat all the same stuff you've already said.

If it's in the application, and you talked about it in the interview, then we're not sure what the value is in repeating yourself again. You could highlight what you feel are the key strengths of your profile, but you should've covered those explicitly several times already. This is a chance for you to cover new territory if needed – or, to discuss any glitches from the interview experience itself.

Another key strategy: If you have learned something new about Harvard since the time you submitted your application, and you didn't get to go into it in depth during the interview, this is a great place to mention it. If you had an insightful conversation with an alumni, if you made friends with a student, if you had some incredible moment during your campus visit, then feel free to describe that here.

And most definitely, if you've accomplished new and different things in your life since you originally submitted the application, present them here.

This is why you should be continuously seeking out new challenges all along. It would be very impressive if you could give the adcom new data at this stage that further reinforces your strengths and "habit of leadership."

The structured approach we offered on page 48 should steer you in the right direction for this deliverable, too.

What to Do Next

Despite the fact that we've managed to go on for 77 pages (!!!), this is not meant as an end-all, be-all guide on everything about Harvard. It's a starting point. You have to do a lot of legwork on your own. This guide should be just the beginning of your research. You need to be talking to people, and ideally traveling to Boston and sitting in on a class and getting in front of the admissions committee to learn what HBS is really all about. It's true: The HBS adcom is very clear in stating that visiting campus is not a pre-requisite of admission. But it can only help.

Luckily Harvard now offers webinars as an introduction to the application. You can find one of them here:

http://www.hbs.edu/about/video.aspx?v=1_vordi6dz

A lot of the advice offered in this Guide was taken directly from comments made by Dee Leopold in such settings (the rest is distilled from our years of experience watching people go through the process and seeing what they submitted, and how it turned out). A webinar is no substitute for visiting but it's a bare-minimum exercise. Watch that video, or even better, participate in one of them in real time and have your questions answered in a chat.

Want more tips? The Harvard Essay Questions page on essaysnark.com has lots. Swing by the EssaySnark blahg to ask a question, or drop us an email at gethelpnow@essaysnark.com (or find EssaySnark on Twitter) to inquire about our specialized MBA admissions consulting services for Harvard, Wharton, LBS, and all the other top bschools of the world.